THE *Bride's*
SEWING BOOK

THE Bride's
SEWING BOOK

ANN LADBURY

Stanley Paul
London Melbourne Sydney Auckland Johannesburg

Stanley Paul & Co. Ltd

An imprint of the Hutchinson Publishing Group
17–21 Conway Street, London W1P 6JD

Hutchinson Publishing Group (Australia) Pty Ltd
PO Box 496, 16–22 Church Street, Hawthorne, Melbourne,
Victoria 3122

Hutchinson Group (NZ) Ltd
32–34 View Road, PO Box 40–086, Glenfield, Auckland 10

Hutchinson Group (SA) Ptd Ltd
PO Box 337, Bergvlei 2012, South Africa

First published 1985
© Ann Ladbury 1985

Set in Linotron Ehrhardt by
Wyvern Typesetting Limited, Bristol

Printed and bound in Great Britain by
Anchor Brendon Ltd, Tiptree, Essex

Ladbury, Ann
    Bride's sewing book.
    1. Wedding costume   2. Dressmaking
    I. Title
    646.4'7   TT515
    ISBN 0 09 159691 2

Tissue patterns printed by Maudella Patterns Co. Ltd
Line illustrations by Jil Shipley
Fashion drawings by Joan Corlass

Cover: A dream of a bride – her dress features a
smocked bodice panel bordered by a trellis of
ribbon studded with pearls. Her young bridesmaid
wears a dress with long sleeves and long skirt with
wide crisp sash. Apply the ruffles to the skirt
before joining it to the bodice, finishing both frill
edges before gathering

Contents

I am very grateful to Myra Davidson, whose daughter got married at just the right time. Also to Kate Beith, Doris Lawrence, Marmie Vergo and Cynthia Hitchen. Special thanks to Cheryl Owen for the patterns, to the friend with the word processor and to the many people who contributed stories if not ideas

Introduction

This book introduces to you a novel way of planning a wedding. With it you can not only *make* the dresses but you can actually design them too. You can select from the sketches or you can combine any of the various features to make your own unique design.

The bride's reason for making – or having made – the wedding dress, may be that she cannot find what she wants ready made at a price she can afford to pay; or that she wants something individual; or that she wants the bridesmaids to be dressed alike no matter what their size. This book solves all those problems and more.

At the back of the book are full-size tissue pattern pieces sized, for adults 8–18 and for children, age 5–10. You will find an assortment of bodices, skirts, sleeves, frills that all fit together in the Mix and Match section beginning on page 12.

At the start of the book there is a diary to help you get it all done in time.

In the middle there are three major sections offering masses of information and tips, including:

a glossary of bridal fabrics and how to sew them;

an A–Z of all the sewing techniques you need; over 20 decorative processes that you can add wherever you wish.

Also, outlines of several delightful motifs for you to trace – select one as your wedding theme and use it on the cake and stationery as well as the clothes.

And, in addition to all this, there are beautiful illustrations of exquisite accessories for all the clothes – even using them on guests' hats and bags.

If you have not made anything like this before you may be nervous but the book takes away the worry. You may not have handled bridal fabrics previously but the numerous tips will make it easier. It is probably the biggest project you have ever tackled, certainly it is the most important. The book will steer you through.

There is no limit to what you can achieve depending on your skill and the time available. Your best efforts will go into it and you will be justly proud of the results.

DESIGN YOUR OWN WEDDING

With the aid of this exciting book you can not only design the dress that is perfect for you and everything you dreamed of – you can plan the whole wedding group. Before even buying the fabric, you can see exactly how your wedding will appear in the photographs.

Design the bridal dress first, then add the bridesmaids and attendants in styles to complement the bride, repeating the major features, accessories and embellishments. There are also short styles for the bride's mother or other prominent guests. Moreover, the basis of your trousseau is here too: a dress for going away; a kimono; an all-in-one suit as nightwear or lingerie and a strapless dress for evenings.

Designing the Wedding Clothes

All you have to do is simply trace off the outlines illustrated and dress the model. Begin by tracing the model girl, then select a bodice and skirt to trace and cut out. Trace several sleeves and decorative features and add these in turn to the dress. Interchange the bodice styles and skirts, see how the dress will look from the back, select any of the features or even draw and cut out your own designs. Let your imagination run riot! (See pages 12–18).

Bear in mind the time of year when the wedding will be taking place. If the ceremony is to be in a church, take into account any views they might have on decorum. You may have an idea about the type of fabric you want to use; it is a good idea to collect some swatches before embarking on designing.

Bridesmaids' dresses can be designed in the same way; you will find that the pattern pieces for sleeves, bodices and skirts are interchangeable. Then line up the entourage and look at the overall effect, making sure you have a complete picture. This does not mean they all have to look the same, but it is important to ensure that the outlines and main features are complementary.

Next add some colour. It helps to start with a paint colour chart – cut out some shades and arrange them on the dressed models. When you have narrowed down your choice, either paint the models or cut out pieces of coloured fabric to fix on to them.

Add touches of contrast where you plan to have them in the way of flowers, head-dresses, ribbons and so on. Change the colours, features and style until you are happy with the overall effect. Fasten together the features that make up each outfit and keep these for reference while the dresses are being made.

When all the decisions have been made, make a list of what has to be bought and complete the chart below to use as a checklist, ticking off each item as it is acquired. Fabric quantities and basic haberdashery requirements are given in the charts beginning on p. 112 but remember to add your own decorative items.

HOW TO USE THE PATTERNS

Included with the book are full-size multi-size paper patterns from 8 to 18 for three bodices, two sleeves and a skirt for adults, plus bodice, sleeve and skirt size for children. Accessories and simple shapes like frills are given as measurements to be followed or diagram patterns to be scaled up.

Ease of movement has been allowed for on all pieces, so select the size you require by consulting the measurement chart and not by measuring the pattern.

A seam allowance of 1.5cm ($\frac{5}{8}$in) is included on all seam edges, but you will be able to adjust this if necessary at fitting.

The amounts allowed for hems are indicated on each piece. Do not include this when adjusting the length of the pattern pieces. If you decide to finish edges by using binding or a separate facing, the hem allowances will be trimmed off.

Locate the pattern pieces you need for the chosen design and cut roughly round each one to separate it from the main sheet. If the pattern is to be used once only, trim each piece again on the line indicating the size you require. If it is to be retained, make a copy using soft sew-in Vilene, pattern paper or greaseproof paper, joining pieces with tape if necessary. Put the Vilene or paper over the pattern and trace the outline using a felt pen. Cut out each piece. Label the pieces with the size, number and name and grain line and also mark notches, balance marks, gathering points etc. A pattern made from Vilene can be tacked up and fitted, then adjusted, taken apart and finally used for cutting out the fabric.

If the pattern piece you want is shown as a diagram on squared grid, you will need a sheet of squared pattern paper: a sheet of plain paper on which you have ruled lines 2.5cm (1in) apart, or a piece of soft sew-in Vilene on top of a cutting board which has squares marked on it. Transfer the shape shown in the book, carefully traversing each square.

Should the pattern piece you wish to use be given in the form of measurements, lay out the fabric as shown in the illustration and – using chalk pencil and a ruler and tape measure – draw the shape desired. If you are particularly nervous of doing this directly on to the fabric, make a paper or Vilene pattern first.

> *If making more than one dress, write the appropriate name on each pattern piece and also tack a name label on to the edge of each piece of fabric as it is cut out.*

Making up the designs

THE PATTERNS   There are three bodices and two sleeves, with numerous possible computations and variations. The skirt pattern provided is one panel that can be used several times to make a skirt as full as is practicable. For instance, in a soft satin or crêpe eight panels could be used, but six would be sufficient in a thick or stiff fabric or if the style incorporates frills. If chiffon or voile is used, ten panels could be joined for the overskirt, but in velvet probably four would be the maximum. Join three panels for a petticoat. If two fabrics are layered the overskirt can be fuller than the underskirt.

After cutting out all the pieces you require, mark centre front, balance marks, dots, zip points, placement lines and so on.

SIZES   The adult patterns are multi-size from 8 to 18. Cut out or trace the pieces you decide to use.

FRILLS   Measurements only are given for frills, as these are made from straight pieces of fabric. The measurements are given for pieces 90cm (36in) wide. If your fabric is wider, it is easy enough to re-calculate the number of pieces you need to cut and join.

ZIP   The zip is inserted in the left side of all the adult dresses as it is less obvious here and allows for more variation in style. If you have a special reason for wanting it in the back, you will need a longer zip than quoted.

LINING   A loose lining is not usually necessary if the dress has a petticoat and often mounting is more appropriate (see page 45). If you wish to line any of the dresses, use the same pattern pieces and simply make an extra skirt and bodice. Put the skirt lining inside the skirt, wrong sides together, and gather up both edges together. Join to the bodice, then use the lining bodice to finish the neck edge and omit the neck facing. Stitch bodice and lining together round the neck; trim and snip the edges and turn the lining to the inside. Press the neck edge. Set the zip into the outer fabric only and use the edge of the lining, turned under, to neaten the waist seam and to cover the zip tape. At armholes, baste bodice and lining together, set in the sleeves – stitching through both layers – and trim and neaten all edges together.

HABERDASHERY   Basic items are listed for each design, including a length of tape for holding the gathers in the skirt. It is difficult to calculate how much thread will be required, but no fewer than six 100-metre reels should be allowed for a long dress, more if much decorative stitching is involved.

SELECTION OF DESIGNS   We have combined various features in many different ways to give you some idea of what is possible (see pp. 11–18). If you wish to make up one of these you will find instructions in the text, and also the fabric and haberdashery requirements for each of those designs. Refer to the Techniques section of the book for details of processes involved.

However, many more designs can be made; further variations are sketched throughout the text. Having planned your own variation, make a list of haberdashery and calculate the fabric quantity by adding together the amounts shown for each feature – adding extra for bows, large quantities of rouleau and so on.

THREAD   It may be wise to try out a couple of different types of thread on scraps of dress fabric before deciding which is most suitable.

The choice rests between the following: spun polyester thread e.g. Drima, which is fine, has plenty of stretch and will sew on all fabrics, whatever the fibre content.

Mercerized cotton e.g. Super Sheen which is a soft traditional thread. Use this on fabrics made from natural fibres only. You may also find you prefer it to polyester for hand sewing. Some older sewing machines prefer this thread.

Core-spun thread e.g. Duet. This is a strong thread with some stretch. It has a polyester core but fine cotton on the outside. It is suitable for all fabrics, for both hand and machine stitching but it has a less lustrous surface than other threads. This is the thread to use if you have the problem of skipped stitches with polyester thread.

Silk e.g. Faro-Seta. Soft, strong thread for use on silk fabrics, it is thicker than other threads. Can be used for fine hand embroidery instead of Anchor Stranded Embroidery Thread.

If the fabric is synthetic – i.e. polyester, nylon, acrylic, not cotton, silk, viscose – you can control fraying by singeing the edges. Hold the edge above a candle flame (not roaring gas) and it will melt slightly. Do try out this technique on scraps of fabric first!

It is worth buying an extra half metre of fabric in case the bride changes her mind about the style of bodice, sleeves, etc. Having this extra material means also that you can experiment with techniques, particularly frills; it is very difficult to guess how much fullness is required.

Wedding diary

A great deal depends upon how far in advance you are able to plan your wedding. However, bearing in mind that some brides will have only weeks in which to arrange everything, whereas others anticipate a long engagement, you must to some degree draw up your own individual schedule. Nevertheless it is always good sense first of all to book the wedding date with the vicar or minister of your parish, or with the register office, then to make arrangements for the reception, cars, photographer, flowers and cake; this leaves your mind clear and free to get on with 'dressing' the wedding. The amount of time that you can allocate to sewing will give you an indication as to how elaborate the dresses can be. Also, you must ascertain how much help you will have with making any of them.

Opposite is a month-by-month diary to guide and help you plan the sewing for your own individual wedding.

Note

If you have less than six months in which to prepare for your wedding, it is best to 'bundle' your sewing and – instead of concentrating on one garment at a time – get everything cut out, allocate space for each dress and have a sheet for each one so that it remains covered when you are not working on it.

Remember that cutting out requires time and patience, otherwise mistakes can be made. Make sure that you are free to cut out a complete garment each time. When all of them have been cut out, concentrate on marking dots and balance marks.

Next tack the bodices of all dresses, ready for a fitting. When this is satisfactory, do all the machining at one sitting and then the pressing. In this way you save time otherwise spent getting yourself and your equipment organised for each separate process on each garment. Then sit down and consider the processes you have to work through. List all the short

cuts you could make and where aids such as Wundaweb and basting tape could be utilized. Try to streamline the processes; for instance, select the easiest type of sleeve opening and use that method only on all dresses, no matter what the style.

If you have to tackle a process that is new to you or one you have not used for some time, make a sample, then you will not have to waste time going slowly on the actual garments.

The long seams of skirts can merely be pinned, but bear in mind that the machining must be done from the hemline to the waist and place the pins from the raw edges inwards.

When time is extra-short, literally everything can be done by the machine: even hems look better machined than hastily hand-sewn and can still be decorative.

6 MONTHS Decide on styles and fabrics for the bride, bridesmaids and any other attendants. Check whether bride's mother is buying or making her own outfit. Don't forget new bras too, so that these can be worn for fitting right from the start — and wedding shoes must be bought — essential for getting hem lengths correct. Remember to get all notions now and have a separate box for each garment so that there are no mix-ups later.

5 MONTHS If responsible for making bride's mother's dress, now is the time to finish it and check that her accessories have been bought. This leaves the field clear to concentrate on bride's and bridesmaid's outfits.

4 MONTHS Should now have clear picture in mind of how bride's dress will look, so that adult bridesmaids' dresses can be got under way — after all, she is the star and they play supporting roles! — Though best to leave finishing hems until last, when all the dresses are completed. Can leave young bridesmaids' dresses to be started about six weeks before the day — hopefully this avoids finding they have all grown about six inches when it comes to the final fitting!

3 MONTHS Time to start the bride's dress — not forgetting the petticoat, which will be required for all fittings. If smocked style is chosen, smocking sections could be prepared by now — time permitting. Best to begin looking for going-away and honeymoon outfits too, as it's bound to take some time getting just what is wanted.

2 MONTHS Bodice of wedding dress ought to be completed and tacked to the skirt ready for a fitting. Double check on petticoat, bras and shoes too, otherwise appointment for fitting will be a waste of time for everyone!

6 WEEKS D-Day to start small bridesmaids' dresses — and was that small nephew persuaded to be a page boy?

1 MONTH Provided schedule has been maintained, should be possible to complete machining and making up of bride's dress, ready for final hemline fitting next week. Also do check on all other sewing!

3 WEEKS Fingers crossed for final fitting! Should only have hem to complete after this, unless bride has lost weight with pre-wedding nerves.

2 WEEKS Zero hour for completing all hemlines.

1 WEEK Everything should be done by now — except for last few hand stitches on bride's dress which are always supposed to be done on the wedding day itself. This ancient tradition is said to sew in luck for the bride, but best to leave a piece of sewing in an unobtrusive place where last-minute nerves cannot spoil anything. Hemming round an armhole is a good idea — certainly not the zip!

Mix and match

panel bodice with single frill

panel bodice with double frill

V-neck bodice (back)

plain bodice (back)

V-neck bodice

plain bodice

panel bodice with
shoulder flounce

panel bodice

panel bodice with
shoulder flounce (back)

panel bodice (back)

panel bodice
(sweetheart neckline)

panel bodice with
square neck (back)

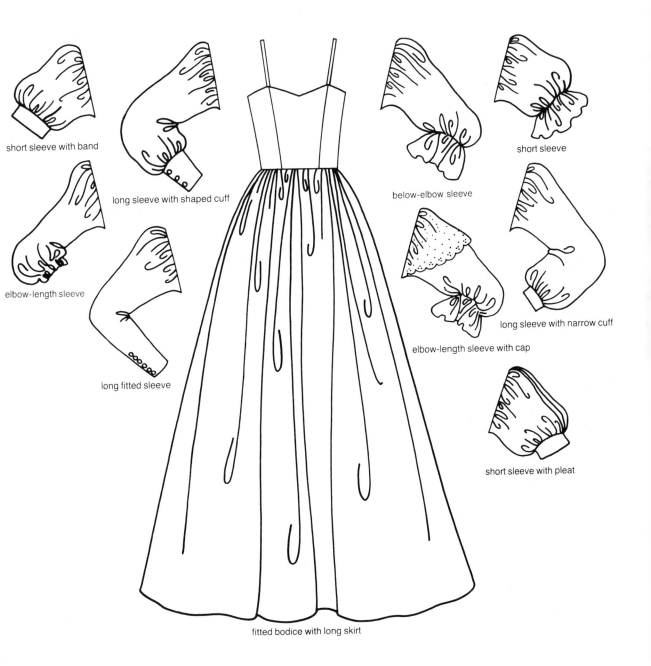

short sleeve with band

long sleeve with shaped cuff

elbow-length sleeve

long fitted sleeve

short sleeve

below-elbow sleeve

long sleeve with narrow cuff

elbow-length sleeve with cap

short sleeve with pleat

fitted bodice with long skirt

long skirt with peplum

short skirt with frill

short tiered skirt

long skirt

short skirt

long tiered skirt

long skirt with double frills

Try to allocate the money at your disposal. The price of fabric varies enormously and you can pay as much or as little as you like, but the extras such as veil, head-dress, shoes, lace edgings, beads, boning, thread and lining will make it all cost considerably more than you expect.

a selection of bows

floating panels

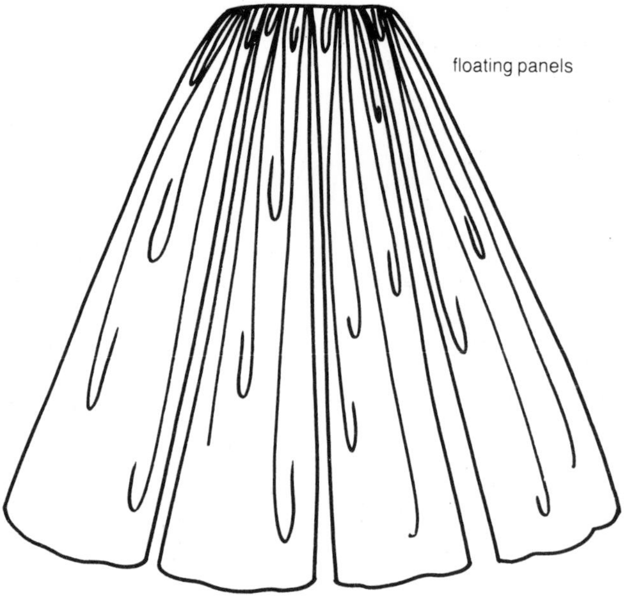

long skirt with deep frill

back view of veil

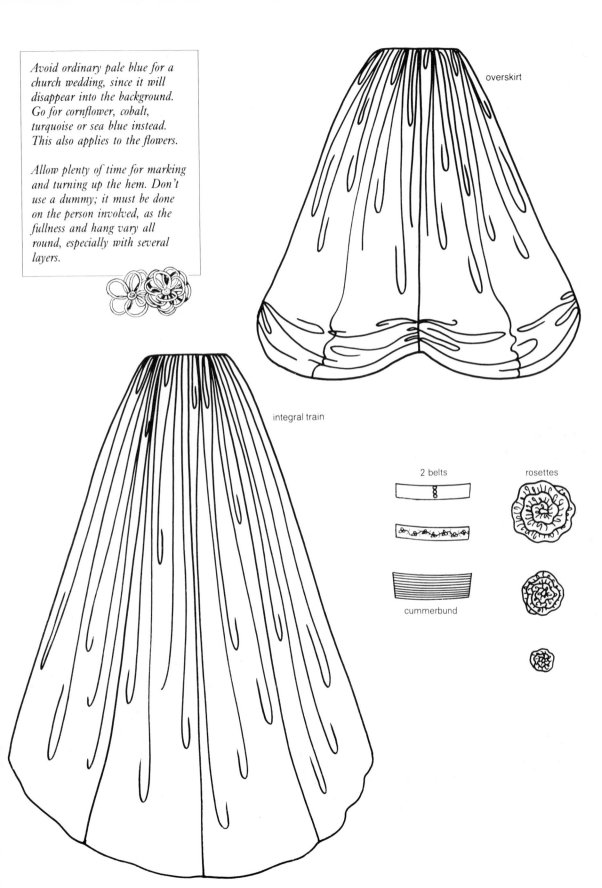

Avoid ordinary pale blue for a church wedding, since it will disappear into the background. Go for cornflower, cobalt, turquoise or sea blue instead. This also applies to the flowers.

Allow plenty of time for marking and turning up the hem. Don't use a dummy; it must be done on the person involved, as the fullness and hang vary all round, especially with several layers.

overskirt

integral train

2 belts

rosettes

cummerbund

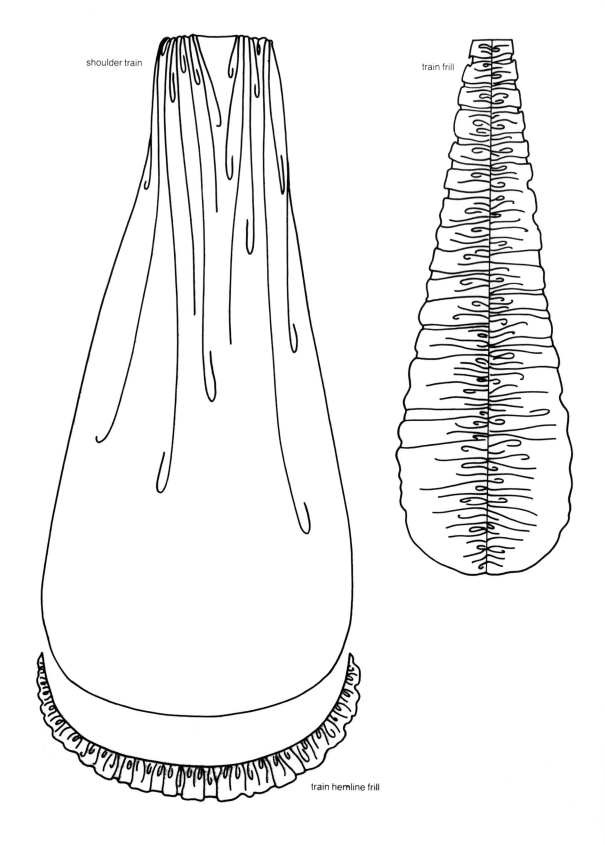

shoulder train

train frill

train hemline frill

Fabric glossary

Acetate satin

Medium weight lustrous satin. Creases slightly, frays. Inexpensive. Dry-clean only. A good base fabric for lace, chiffon etc., or for dense decoration. The best weight of satin to use for piping seams in another fabric.

SEAMS: Plain open.
HEMS: Deep hand-stitched or narrow machined or line to edge.
FEATURES: Quilting, tucks, ribbon embroidery, ruched narrow lace.
MACHINE NEEDLE: 80–11, possibly Universal (scarf)
STITCH: Medium.
INTERFACING: Light sew-in Vilene.
PRESS: Warm iron.

Antung silk

Crisp plain weave silk, often with woven patterns. One of the cheapest silks. Good as a base for chiffon, organza etc., and for petticoats and special lining.

SEAMS: Plain open.
HEMS: Deep or narrow hand-sewn or machined.
FEATURES: Top stitching, binding, tucks, beading, ruching.
MACHINE NEEDLE: 80–11.
STITCH: Medium.
INTERFACING: Sew-in Vilene or organdie.
PRESS: Warm iron.

Broderie anglais

Sometimes called Eyelet embroidery. Austrian cotton or 35% cotton, 65% polyester. Design may be all-over or border. If the latter, plan the dress design carefully. Pretty fabric; the beauty is in the design, so keep to full gathered styles and added ribbons. Line with self colour or strong contrast. Washable, will dye, varies in price.

SEAMS: French, narrow.
HEMS: Narrow or line to edge; broderie anglais edgings.
FEATURES: Ribbons, frills: Dolly bags.
MACHINE NEEDLE: 80–11.
STITCH: Medium.
INTERFACING: Soft iron-on but make sure it does not show.
PRESS: Hot iron or steam iron.

Brocade

Can be polyester or acetate but the most beautiful are 100% silk. Crisp and stiff, the beauty is in the design which will feature a number of matt and shiny yarns and also often gold or silver. Dry-clean only. Price varies. Frays easily but not difficult to sew.

SEAMS: Plain open.
HEMS: Deep hand-stitched.
FEATURES: Beading on motifs of fabric; use for wide belt or cummerbund on plain fabrics. Use also for bags.

MACHINE NEEDLE: 80–11.
STITCH: Medium.
INTERFACING: Medium sew-in Vilene.
PRESS: Warm iron.

Chantilly lace

Cotton design on nylon netting. Expensive lace but soft and pretty. Often has scalloped edge that can be cut off and re-joined. Choose under-fabric carefully for best effect. To add body to sleeves etc., mount on to veiling net.

SEAMS: Narrow or match pattern and oversew.
HEMS: Appliqué a matching lace trim, possibly cut from the material if it is suitable in design.
FEATURES: Use for appliqué, bind the edges with satin, add matching lace edging. Ribbons.
MACHINE NEEDLE: 80–11.
STITCH: Medium; small zig-zag.
INTERFACING: Net; organdie.
PRESS: Warm iron or steam iron, on towel.

Cloqué

Soft fabric, 70% viscose, 30% acetate or possibly others; bubbly surface in a regular design formed by tight fine yarns on the back and longer yarns on the top. The beauty is in the design, so choose a simple style and be very controlled with decoration; avoid top stitching. Needs lining.

SEAMS: Plain open.

HEMS: Single turning, zig-zag raw edge, and hem with catch stitch.

FEATURES: Fitted sleeves, add fabric flowers, satin buttons, stand-up collar, Edwardian styles.

MACHINE NEEDLE: 70–9.

STITCH: Medium.

INTERFACING: Soft sew-in Vilene.

PRESS: Cover ironing board with terry towelling – warm iron, light pressure, wrong side only.

Cotton jacquard

Thick cotton fabric with a variety of patterns produced on the surface by the long loose threads or 'floats'. The various parts of the design reflect the light in different ways. Completely opaque; not necessary to line. Washable; would dye. Suitable for sculptured and gathered styles with crisp outline. Creases hardly at all.

SEAMS: Plain open.

HEMS: Deep hand-stitched; Wundaweb.

FEATURES: Piping, binding, top stitching, quilting.

MACHINE NEEDLE: 90–14.

STITCH: Medium.

INTERFACING: Firm iron-on Vilene.

PRESS: Hot iron and damp muslin or steam iron.

Cotton velvet

Firm short pile velvet. The easiest one to sew. Dry-clean only; fairly expensive. Cut all pieces with pile running upwards. Stitch and press in the same direction. Tack seams, but leave thread loose and allow fabric to creep if it wants to. Avoid bulky edges and facings. Needs lining. Lends itself to the addition of contrast texture such as satin.

SEAMS: Plain open. Use dual feed on machine if you have it.

HEMS: Deep hand-sewn.

FEATURES: Quilting, beading. Muffs, bags.

MACHINE NEEDLE: 80–11.

STITCH: Large.

INTERFACING: Soft sew-in Vilene.

PRESS: Warm iron and damp muslin. Press very lightly on wrong side only, with fabric right side down on to the right side of a spare piece of velvet. It is worth cutting a piece to the shape of your sleeve board or ironing board.

Crêpe de chine

Silk. Thin fine, matt luxurious fabric. Soft and floppy, creases. Medium price range. The perfect ground for embroidery and hand work; a good fabric to contrast with lace chiffon and satin.

SEAMS: French narrow.

HEMS: Deep hand-sewn or narrow bound or lace-trimmed.

FEATURES: Tucks, beads, pearls, rouleau, binding, frills.

MACHINE NEEDLE: 90–9.

STITCH: Small.

INTERFACING: Soft sew-in Vilene or organza.

PRESS: Warm iron.

Embroidered net

Also called embroidered flouncing, this is fine nylon net usually embroidered boldly with lustrous viscose yarn. Expensive. Use as an over-fabric. Do not add decoration except beads, pearls etc. Designs are usually too heavy for veils. A good choice if you want an instant fabric; usually a border design with scalloped edge and wide width for long skirts.

SEAMS: Narrow.

HEMS: Narrow zig-zag.

FEATURES: Binding, rouleau, loops in contrast fabric.

MACHINE NEEDLE: 70–9.

STITCH: Small zig-zag.

INTERFACING: Net; organdie.

PRESS: Warm iron.

Façonné

Soft fabric with woven pattern in satin weave, the reverse of which is on the underside. The best is silk in lovely creamy white. Expensive. Creases very little. Use for full draped styles.

SEAMS: French, narrow.

HEMS: Deep or narrow hand-sewn, shell-edge etc.

FEATURES: Quilting, binding, beading, rouleau.

MACHINE NEEDLE: 70–9.

STITCH: Small.

INTERFACING: Soft sew-in Vilene

PRESS: Warm iron.

Flocked nylon voile

A crisp transparent fabric with sparkle. Creases little; washable; inexpensive. Needs lining.

SEAMS: Narrow; use tissue paper if they wrinkle.

HEMS: Narrow machined.

FEATURES: Ruching, binding, single frills stiched down the middle.

MACHINE NEEDLE: 70–9, possibly Universal (scarf).

STITCH: Small.

INTERFACING: None

PRESS: Warm iron.

Moiré

Thick dense fabric with heavy crosswise yarn giving it a ribbed appearance. Has a characteristic water-marked pattern on the right side. Usually acetate or acetate with nylon; can be hand-washed.

SEAMS: Plain open, piped or top stitched.

HEMS: Deep hand-sewn or machined.

FEATURES: Ribbon in contrasting texture, e.g. velvet; binding, piping, beading, pearls, tucks.

MACHINE NEEDLE: 80–11.

STITCH: Medium.

INTERFACING: Medium iron-on Vilene. Wundaweb.

PRESS: Warm iron, steam iron.

Ninghai silk

Heavy wild silk without lustre. Inexpensive. Creases less than other silks. Use as a base for beading etc., and with heavy lace and other contrast textures.

SEAMS: Plain open, piped.

HEMS: Deep hand-sewn or machined.

FEATURES: Top stitching, flat tucks, beading; bind with satin; add satin ribbons.

MACHINE NEEDLE: 80–11.

STITCH: Medium.

INTERFACING: Soft sew-in Vilene or organdie.

PRESS: Warm iron.

Net

Use soft dress net or veiling net for facing and interfacing where other fabrics show. Can also be cut in narrow strips to flat-bind fraying seams without adding bulk. Use also as a top fabric to be beaded, appliquéd etc., or folded double and gathered into narrow ruffles.

SEAMS: Narrow.

HEMS: Narrow zig-zag, rolled or bound.

FEATURES: Double frill, appliqué, beading.

MACHINE NEEDLE: 70–9.

STITCH: Small zig-zag.

INTERFACING: Self fabric.

PRESS: Warm iron.

Nylon georgette

Soft but springy plain or printed fine nylon. Frays. Will gather crisply. Needs lining. Washable, inexpensive.

SEAMS: French; narrow. Use tissue paper if they wrinkle.

HEMS: Narrow machined.

FEATURES: Add ribbons; bound edges, double frills.

MACHINE NEEDLE: 70–9.

STITCH: Small.

INTERFACING: None

PRESS: Warm iron.

Nylon lace

Sometimes labelled 'allover' lace, this is Raschel construction fine ground with a regular design on it. Light weight, suitable for veils as well as over-dress. Not expensive. Spaces between flowers etc. are usually quite large, so choose backing fabric carefully. There may be an edge that you can cut off and rejoin elsewhere, so work out quantities carefully. Washable. Does not crease. Also use for cutting out motifs to apply to plain fabrics and plain net.

SEAMS: Narrow; stitch over tissue paper. Overlap motifs and over-sew or zig-zag.

HEMS: Trim round motif and zig-zag; zig-zag on edge, add narrow lace ruffles.

FEATURES: Bind or pipe with contrast; add ribbons, plain net frills.

MACHINE NEEDLE: 70–9.

STITCH: Medium; small zig-zag.

INTERFACING: Plain net.

PRESS: Warm iron over towel.

Organdie

Similar to organza but crisper and made from cotton. Use for accessories such as crisp collars and bows; also as interfacing for soft, fine fabrics. Handle as organza.

Organza

Fine crisp transparent silk fabric for over-dress, sleeves, veils etc. Creases. Can be expensive. Does not lie flat when gathered, so use same width as under-fabric and gather both materials together. Choose base fabric carefully; those with a design look best, such as moiré. Use the cheaper organza for supporting style features such as sleeves and frills and for petticoats. Can also be used for interfacing light soft fabrics.

SEAMS: Narrow, French.

HEMS: Narrow machined; bound.

FEATURES: Frills, add ribbon, use for bows and sashes.

MACHINE NEEDLE: 70–9.

STITCH: Small.

INTERFACING: Self fabric if required, e.g. cuffs.

PRESS: Warm iron.

Polyester crêpe

Fairly firm, dense, matt fabric, suitable for a wide variety of styles. Very inexpensive, hand washable. A good fabric to use as a base for decorative techniques. Not difficult to sew but seams may wrinkle. Needs lining.

SEAMS: Narrow. Edges of seams will show through.

HEMS: Narrow.

FEATURES: Binding, beading, pearls, quilting, rouleau. Make bows, flowers.

MACHINE NEEDLE: 70–9 Universal (scarf).

STITCH: Small.

INTERFACING: Soft sew-in Vilene.

PRESS: Warm iron. Do not press over neatened edges.

Polyester crêpe de chine

Fine springy fabric in 'good' white. Frays little, washable.

Needs lining. Inexpensive enough to be used as a lining fabric or as under-fabric for lace etc. Soft and floppy, so choose drapy styles; any stiff petticoat etc. will show through. Not particularly easy to sew.

SEAMS: Narrow or French.
HEMS: Narrow machined.
FEATURES: Binding, frills, appliqué.
MACHINE NEEDLE: 80–11 Universal (scarf).
STITCH: Medium; small zig-zag.
INTERFACING: Soft sew-in Vilene.
PRESS: Warm iron or steam iron.

Polyester crêpe georgette

Georgette made from crêpe yarns, which makes it a soft floppy fabric of a good weight. Hangs and drapes well. Hand washable, inexpensive. Mixes well with contrast texture such as satin, but take care to match whites. Use for flowers, sashes.

SEAMS: French; narrow.
HEMS: Narrow machined; rolled.
FEATURES: Binding, ruching, frills, ruffles, rouleau.
MACHINE NEEDLE: 70–9.
STITCH: Small.
INTERFACING: Polyester organza.
PRESS: Warm iron.

Polyester jacquard satin

Soft fabric, with designs in relief which can be embellished with pearls, beads etc. Does not crease; hand washable; inexpensive. Needs lining. Hemlines will shadow, so be prepared to cover on right side with piping etc.

SEAMS: Narrow. Stitch on tissue paper if they wrinkle.
HEMS: Deep hand stitched.
FEATURES: Frills, piping, beading, rouleau.

MACHINE NEEDLE: 70–9 Universal (scarf).
STITCH: Small.
INTERFACING: Soft sew-in Vilene.
PRESS: Warm iron.

Polyester jersey

Fine knitted fabric. Washable, easy to sew, does not fray or crease. Wide width, inexpensive. Needs lining. Use for full gathered unfussy styles. Cut one-way.

SEAMS: Plain open or narrow.
HEMS: Narrow machined or fluted.
FEATURES: Top stitching, smocking, ruching, piping.
MACHINE NEEDLE: 70–9 Ball point. If stitches miss, try Universal needle; put paper under fabric, on top also if necessary.
STITCH: Medium zig-zag.
INTERFACING: Soft sew-in Vilene.
PRESS: Warm iron or steam iron.

Polyester organza

Crisp, inexpensive transparent fabric. Does not crease, hand washable. Use as over-fabric or for additional features such as a big sash, bows, collars, etc. Use as interfacing in fine light synthetic fabrics.

SEAMS: Narrow.
HEMS: Narrow machined.
FEATURES: Double frills, add ribbon. Use for making flowers.
MACHINE NEEDLE: 70–9.
STITCH: Small.
INTERFACING: Self fabric.
PRESS: Warm iron.

Polyester taffeta

Crisp, closely woven fabric. Creases slightly. Not expensive. An excellent choice as a base fabric for decorative techniques.

May have water-mark pattern on it.

SEAMS: Plain open.
HEMS: Narrow; deep hems will shadow.
FEATURES: Tucks, beading, piping, pearls, frills, ruffles, bows, sashes.
MACHINE NEEDLE: 70–9 Universal (scarf).
STITCH: Medium.
INTERFACING: Soft sew-in Vilene.
PRESS: Warm iron. Do not press over neatened edges.

Polyester voile

Soft see-through fabric. Choose one with a fine weave – a density of yarns per centimetre in each direction – and it will not fray too badly or be too difficult to handle. Drapes well, does not crease. May not be dead white. Inexpensive. Can be hand-washed.

SEAMS: French; narrow.
HEMS: Narrow, shell, picot, rolled, bound.
FEATURES: Single or double full frill and flounces, bows, sashes.
MACHINE NEEDLE: 70–9.
STITCH: Small.
INTERFACING: None.
PRESS: Medium iron, use damp muslin.

Rayon satin

Thick, closely woven crisp satin with highly lustrous surface. Completely opaque but improved by lining. Creases little. Fabric is self-supporting; use for sculptured styles or as a base for lace. Expensive. Beware of pin-marks.

SEAMS: Plain open.
HEMS: Deep hand-stitched but will probably show: be prepared to cover line with ribbon, lace ruffles, etc.

FEATURES: Use for making roses, cummerbunds, clutch bags, beading, quilting.
MACHINE NEEDLE: 90–14, possibly Universal (scarf).
STITCH: Large.
INTERFACING: Firm iron-on Vilene. Wundaweb.
PRESS: Warm dry iron or steam iron. Do not press over neatened seams or bulky edges.

Rayon taffeta

An inexpensive lining fabric suitable in weight for almost all medium to heavy top fabrics. Use for petticoats too. Not washable.

SEAMS: French; narrow.
HEMS: Narrow machined.
MACHINE NEEDLE: 70–9.
STITCH: Small.
PRESS: Warm iron or steam iron.

Satin stripe cotton voile

Fresh soft cotton for unsophisticated full styles with full sleeves and gathered skirts. Lends itself to simple decoration and the addition of colour in the form of ribbons. Washable; will dye. Creases, but as with almost any beautiful fabric it will not detract from it. Needs lining.

SEAMS: French; narrow.
HEMS: Deep hems will show. Add frills; cover hem line with ribbon.
FEATURES: Smocking, tucks, ribbons, embroidered stripes. Bind edges or machine stitch.
MACHINE NEEDLE: 80–11.
STITCH: Small to medium.
INTERFACING: Organdie, soft sew-in Vilene.
PRESS: Hot iron or steam iron.

Silk chiffon

Soft floaty fabric, plain or printed. Do not wash. Expensive; does not crease. For elegant styles such as those with very full sleeves, cape collars, full skirts. Complement it with a good under-fabric. Use it with strapless bodice beneath. Not easy to sew; cannot be hurried.

SEAMS: French.
HEMS: Narrow rolled or shell edge; fine zig-zag or add ribbon.
FEATURES: Binding, sashes, deep neckline frills.
MACHINE NEEDLE: 70–9.
STITCH: Small.
INTERFACING: Silk organza.
PRESS: Warm iron.

Silk habutai

Inexpensive thin silk for lining.

SEAMS: French; narrow.
HEMS: Deep, narrow machined, shell-edge or lace edged.
MACHINE NEEDLE: 70–9.
STITCH: Small.
PRESS: Warm iron.

Silk jacquard

Soft crêpe with satin design and the effect reversed on the under side. Can be used with either side uppermost. Does not crease; elegant; expensive. Restrict decoration, in order to retain the beauty of the fabric.

SEAMS: French.
HEMS: Deep hems will shadow. Use narrow hand-sewn hems.
FEATURES: Binding, double frills.
MACHINE NEEDLE: 70–9.
STITCH: Small.
INTERFACING: Soft sew-in Vilene; organza.
PRESS: Warm iron.

Silk satin

Soft, luxurious, beautiful creamy fabric. Also called slipper satin. Creases very little. Expensive. Worthy of care and fine hand-sewing. Takes time, not to be hurried. Frays little, drapes and gathers well. Needs lining.

SEAMS: French.
HEMS: Deep or narrow hand-sewn.
FEATURES: Narrow binding, quilting, beading, piping, rouleau.
MACHINE NEEDLE: 70–9.
STITCH: Small.
INTERFACING: Soft sew-in Vilene.
PRESS: Warm/medium iron.

Silk taffeta

Sometimes called paper taffeta, this is a fine and lovely plain-weave crisp silk. It is characterized by always having a faintly crumpled uneven appearance caused by the closeness of the weave and reflection of light. Dry-clean only. Expensive. For bouffant styles with deep frills. A good base for decoration. Looks good with other colours, pale ribbon, piping etc. Needs lining.

SEAMS: Plain open.
HEMS: Narrow or deep; hemline may be covered with decoration.
FEATURES: Piping, beading, pearls, frills, ruffles, sashes, tucks, top stitching, bows.
MACHINE NEEDLE: 70–9 Universal (scarf).
STITCH: Small.
INTERFACING: Soft sew-in Vilene; organdie.
PRESS: Warm iron.

Spotted rayon organza

Lovely fine crisp Swiss fabric with raised satin-stitched spots. Sometimes called Point d'esprit. Expensive but stylish and distinctive. Use over taffeta. Excellent over a strapless bodice.

SEAMS: French; narrow.

HEMS: Narrow, zig-zag, rolled, bound.
FEATURES: Binding, frills, add covered buttons.
MACHINE NEEDLE: 70–9.
STITCH: Small.
INTERFACING: None.
PRESS: Warm iron.

Spun silk

Matt plain-weave creamy silk. Suitable for most styles. Hand wash. Medium priced. Needs lining, creases little. An excellent choice if you want to do your own decoration. The perfect base for many techniques. As a contrast add satin features, flowers etc.

SEAMS: Plain open.
HEMS: Deep hand-sewn.
FEATURES: Add satin binding. Beading, quilting, smocking, embroidery, painting, top stitching.
MACHINE NEEDLE: 70–9.
STITCH: Small.
INTERFACING: Soft sew-in Vilene; organdie.
PRESS: Warm iron. Do not press over neatened edges.

Suede-finish satin

Loose-weave polyester satin with matt surface. Use as a base fabric for lace etc., or add plenty of decoration. Inexpensive. Beware pin-marks. Does not crease. Suitable for fabric roses.

SEAMS: Plain open.
HEMS: Deep hand-sewn or narrow machined. Wundaweb.
FEATURES: Deep single frills and ruffles, beading, appliqué. Use for stiffened cummerbund.
MACHINE NEEDLE: 80–11.
STITCH: Medium.
INTERFACING: Soft iron-on Vilene.
PRESS: Warm dry iron or steam iron but not over stitched seam edges or ridges.

Swiss voile

Fine transparent plain weave 100% cotton; fresh simple fabric. Use for full styles, big sleeves and dainty decoration. Line with another fabric, not a lining fabric. Washable, will dye. Frays easily, not difficult to sew.

SEAMS: French.
HEMS: Narrow or deep, double hems or double frills.
FEATURES: Shadow work, ribbon embroidery, smocking.
MACHINE NEEDLE: 80–11.
STITCH: Medium.
INTERFACING: None.
PRESS: Hot iron or steam iron.

Thai silk

Thick heavy rough-surfaced silk. Expensive, but beautiful, with distinctive lustre. Dry-clean only; needs lining. Frays, but not difficult to sew. Crisp enough for big sleeves, crinoline skirts.

SEAMS: Plain open.
HEMS: Deep hand-sewn.
FEATURES: Deep frills, top stitching, beads, pearls, bold embroidery, quilting.
MACHINE NEEDLE: 80–11.
STITCH: Medium.
INTERFACING: Medium sew-in Vilene. Wundaweb.
PRESS: Warm iron. Do not press over neatened edges.

Tussah

Medium weight matt silk, characterized by thicker crosswise, slightly slubbed yarns. Creases. A very inexpensive variety of silk. Use on its own, with satin trim in contrast colours, or with heavy lace.

SEAMS: Plain open; piped.
HEMS: Deep hand-sewn or machined.
FEATURES: Top stitching, flat tucks, beading, appliqué.
MACHINE NEEDLE: 80–11.
STITCH: Medium.
INTERFACING: Soft sew-in Vilene or organdie.
PRESS: Warm iron.

Voile

Lightweight sheer plain-weave fabric with good draping qualities. May be cotton, polyester, nylon or a mixture of fibres. Use for over-dresses, sheer sleeves. May have woven pattern of stripes, checks etc. Spotted voile is excellent for smocking (see page 00).

SEAMS: French; narrow.
HEMS: Narrow machined, shell edge, bound.
FEATURES: Pin tucks, smocking, hand embroidery, frills.
MACHINE NEEDLE: 70–9.
STITCH: Small.
INTERFACING: None.
PRESS: Steam iron or warm iron.

Wild silk

Crisp creamy silk, often Swiss, with characteristic uneven yarns and slightly crushed appearance in wear. Brought to popularity by Princess Diana; use it for full bouffant styles with extravagant frills and bows. Needs lining. Not difficult to sew. Expensive but worth it.

SEAMS: Plain open.
HEMS: Deep hand-stitched.
FEATURES: Beads, quilting, piping.
MACHINE NEEDLE: 80–11.
STITCH: Medium.
INTERFACING: Medium sew-in Vilene; organza.
PRESS: Warm iron.

BIAS FABRIC

If you need long pieces of bias fabric, cut it in one long strip as follows:

Use a rectangle of fabric – half a metre, half a yard or whatever you have available – and mark some bias lines the width required at an angle of 45 degrees. Mark on the wrong side of the fabric, using tailor's chalk, fabric pen,

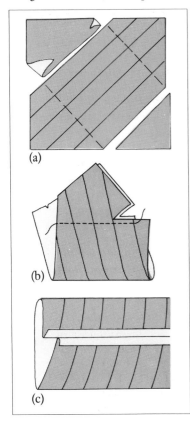

(a)

(b)

(c)

etc. Cut off the unmarked opposite corners (a). Fold the fabric right sides together; place the cut edges together, but so that the width of one strip is left extending. Stitch the join and press open (b). Cut the strip, cutting round and round the tube (c).

BINDING

Bind edges of hems, frills, sleeves, petticoats with bought satin binding; or use bias strips which can be of matching or contrast fabric. If you use fabric, it is worth buying a tool called a Tape Maker. Cut the bias to the width given on the package and pass it through the Tape Maker, pressing it as it emerges; it is then folded ready for use. Use these bindings singly. No seam allowance is needed on the garment edge, so if the size of the piece is critical trim off 1.5cm (⅝in) before you start.

Single binding

Attach by machine to the edge of firm fabric by slotting the binding over the edge and attaching with a small zig-zag stitch (opposite), catching the edge of the binding on top and beneath. It may help to press the binding – folded not quite in half, with the slightly wider edge underneath – to be sure of catching it in the stitching. If you want to add further decoration in the form of machine

embroidery, tack the binding in position first, keeping the tacking away from the edge so that it is not caught in the embroidery.

To attach by machine but hem by hand to finish, open out one fold of binding and tack it to the right side of the garment; machine in the crease. Trim the raw edges a little. Press by pushing the binding to extend, using the toe of the iron on the right side. On the wrong side, bring the binding over on to the machine stitching and tack. Hem into the stitching. Remove tacking and press.

To join bias strips, lay them end to end wrong side up with cut edges together. Pick up each pair of ends and press over a narrow fold. Join the folds. If there are only one or two joins to be made, they can be back-stitched by hand. Press them open and trim off the triangles at the sides. The final join when the binding goes round a continuous edge is difficult to make; it should be made

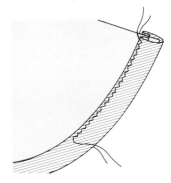

on the straight grain, i.e. at an angle like the others. Stop the stitching attaching the binding 5cm (2in) from the end, fold the garment at that point at an angle of 45 degrees, allowing both ends of binding to extend. Pin the join, but make sure it is correct by opening out the garment again. The binding should lie flat. Stitch the join, trim and press. Complete the stitching. If you find this straight grain join difficult to do, compromise by putting it at an inconspicuous point on the garment and turn in the edges to meet each other. Press the folds. The join will show less if you do not attempt to stitch the folds together.

Double binding

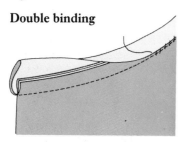

This produces a lovely effect. Use only fine fabrics like chiffon and voile. Make an experimental piece to determine the exact width of strip required, then cut a bias strip of fabric four times the finished width plus two seam allowances of 5mm ($\frac{1}{4}$in). Fold the strip wrong side inside and press. Place on the right side of garment and tack. Machine in place 5mm ($\frac{1}{4}$in) from the edge. Trim the garment edge if necessary. Roll the binding over to the wrong side, bringing the fold on to the machine stitching. Tack in position. Hem into the machine stitches (above).

Joins are difficult to make in double binding after it has been

applied; it is probably best to fold the ends edge to edge and press.

Mitres

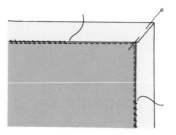

Corners can be mitred by stopping the stitching 2.5cm (1in) from the corner. Fold the binding to meet across the corner, press the folds and lift and join the binding. Trim off the end and complete the stitching. Take care not to stretch the binding when making mitres.

BUTTONS AND LOOPS

Ball buttons

Also called Chinese buttons, these can be used with cord frogging or with rouleau or thread loops; they also make an attractive decoration. Make a long piece of rouleau so that you have plenty to practise with; have it as fine as the fabric will allow. Use soft rouleau or, for firm loops, rouleau filled with piping cord. Cut the rouleau into pieces 10–15cm (4–6in) in length and wind each into a button as shown. Trim the surplus rouleau.

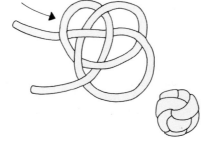

Long sleeves extending into points over the hand easily ride up and wrinkle, so stitch a loop made from rouleau to the hem of the sleeve in line with the wrist opening to slip over the little finger.

Tuck in the raw ends and stitch them flat to the button; making this side the underneath, sew the button to the garment using double thread, waxed, and making a short shank to take the loop. Check that it is firm, as ball buttons tend to wobble.

Button loops

THREAD LOOPS   These are inconspicuous and should be used where only one or at the most two are required. Use thread doubled, waxed and twisted. Attach the button first, then start the loop exactly opposite. Take a double stitch under the edge, bring the needle out on the garment edge, wind it round the button and take a stitch along the garment edge. Make four such loops and stitches, but be sure they are big enough to come over the button, though not so loose that they slip off. Work loop stitch close together along the loop. Finish with two back stitches under the edge. Cut off the knot.

FABRIC LOOPS   Make from filled or soft rouleau. First make an experimental loop in order to obtain exactly the right size to go over the button. To do this, stitch a piece of rouleau to fabric and keep adding an extra line of stitching, making the loop smaller and smaller until it fits closely over the button (opposite top).

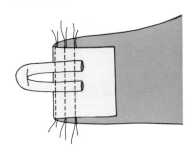

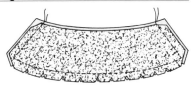

Snip the loop off and cut the required number of pieces that length plus 3cm (1¼in) seam allowance. Space out the buttons on the other side of the opening and mark the positions with fabric pen, but do not sew them on. Transfer these marks to the loop side of the opening on the right side. Pin a length of rouleau to fit round each mark, with the ends level with the raw edge of the garment. Anchor the loops with basting tape, stitch across the loops on the seam allowance. Remove pins. Place the second piece of fabric on top, right side down, and tack. Turn fabric over and stitch, using the first row as a guide. Trim seam allowance and loop ends, roll fabric so loops extend, removing basting tape. Baste along edge of garment. Press edge, using the toe of the iron, but do not press over the rouleau.

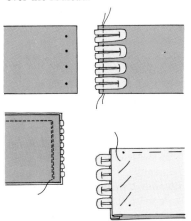

Covered buttons

Send fabric away to have covered buttons made or cover your own using sets of 'Trims' moulds. The buttons can be made using contrast material. Remember to place lining underneath transparent fabrics.

The buttons can be embellished to correspond with other decoration on the dress. Suggestions include: adding pearls or beads, gold or silver embroidery; a cluster of French knots; narrow lace edging gathered up and sewn to the outer edge; a lace or ribbon rosette sewn to the centre of the button.

COLLARS

The collar on the bridesmaid's dress can either match the dress or be made in a contrast such as voile or organdie. A double collar is an attractive feature; a pattern piece for an upper collar is provided. The two can be made from the same fabric, or one from dress fabric and one from contrast such as organdie; alternatively, two different contrasts could be used, for example satin with lace or voile. If you wish to add decoration to the upper collar such as pin tucks, wing needle stitching, a quilted motif or appliqué, mark out the shape of the collar on the fabric, work the decoration and then cut out the collar. Decoration such as beading and hand embroidery should be left until the dress is complete.

Making the collar

INTERFACED COLLAR If the fabric is opaque, cut two collar pieces in soft iron-on Vilene – or four pieces if making double collars – and

press to the wrong side of the fabric, taking care that the straight grain is placed correctly. Mark the balance marks on each piece at neckline edge. Cut two more (or four more) collars from fabric. Place each pair of collar pieces right sides together and baste along the middle. Mark a 1.5cm (⅝in) seam allowance round outer edge of each collar and stitch, stopping 1cm (⅜in) from each corner and changing the stitch to a smaller size to reduce the risk of fraying. Press the stitching flat, then trim the edges down to 5mm (¼in) or less and cut off the corners close to the stitching. It also helps to trim back the interfacing seam allowance inside the collar at the neck edge (above). Turn collars right side out by placing your thumb close to the stitching, sharply pulling one layer of fabric over it, and then gently easing a bodkin point into the corner of the collar to bring the seam right to the edge. If the fabric is one that frays badly, push a very small piece of Wundaweb into the corner; when the collar is pressed the Wundaweb will melt and prevent fraying. Use your fingers to roll the seam to the edge all round,

If you plan to use bias binding for hems, seams etc., or as a casing for elastic, use satin binding as a special touch. Buy a whole reel of it, then you will have enough to make hanging loops, use on bags, edge the veil etc.

then ease the seam to the underside a fraction, i.e. towards the
interfaced layer, and tack near the
edge. Press collar edges lightly
from underside. If you wish to
add lace edging this should be
done now, gathering up the lace
and hemming it to the underside
of the collar. This is easier to do
if you make sure you buy lace
with a thread running along the
edge for pulling up. If you wish to
add narrow ribbon to the collar,
do so now, marking a line 1cm
(⅜in) from the outer edge and
attaching the ribbon with a zig-
zag stitch.

Baste layers of collar together
along neck edge, then remove all
other tacking. Place the collars
together at the centre front and
stick a piece of basting tape across
them 1.5cm (⅝in) from the edge.
For a double collar, join the pairs,
then put upper collar on top of
lower collar, matching balance
marks at neck edges; then
machine stitch round the neck
1.5cm (⅝in) from the edge.

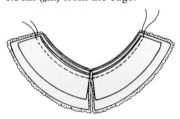

NON-INTERFACED COLLAR   If the
fabric is transparent, do not insert
Vilene. Instead use two layers of
fabric on the top of the collar and
one beneath. In addition to
adding a degree of stiffness, this
will ensure that seam allowances
do not show. Cut out all collar
pieces, baste two together for each
upper section, then make and join
them at the centre front as described above.

An alternative method if you do
not want to use an extra layer of
fabric is to make the seam in the
outer edge inconspicuous. To do
this, stitch round the outer edge
on the seam line with a very small
zig-zag stitch, trim the fabric close
to the stitching, turn collar right
side out, press and stitch the edge
again with either a straight or a
small zig-zag stitch or with a
machine embroidery stitch.

Attaching the collar

This should be done before joining on the skirt. Join shoulder
seams of dress. Collar can be
attached with a bias strip of
fabric, or if the dress is lined use
the lining made up to the same
stage as the dress.

To attach the collar with a bias
strip, cut a piece of fabric on the
cross 2cm (¾in) wide. Press to
stretch it; turn under a narrow
edge along one side and press
again. Place collar to right side of
dress, matching balance marks,
raw edges and centre front and
centre back points. Tack round
neck. Machine stitch for a short
distance 1.5cm (⅝in) from the
edge across the ends of the collar
at the centre back and across the
centre front. If the fabric is very
slippery, stitch right round the
neck. Place bias strip on top of
collar with the unpressed edge

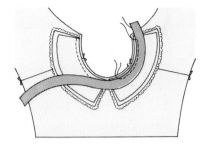

1cm (⅜in) below neck edge, allowing at least 1cm (⅜in) to extend
beyond the centre back edges.
Tack and stitch 5mm (¼in) from
edge of bias, i.e. 1.5cm (⅝in) from
the dress neck edge. Remove all
tackings. Trim seam allowances
and snip frequently all round the
neck. To press, pull the collar out
to extend beyond the dress and
use the toe of the iron to push the
bias strip over towards the inside
of the dress. At centre back, trim
in ends of bias, then tack folded
edge to dress making sure no
wrinkles appear under the collar
on the right side. Hem fold of
bias to dress, slip-stitch ends at
centre back (opposite top).

To attach the collar using the
bodice lining, place collar to right
side of neckline, matching centre
front, centre back and balance
marks and tack. Machine stitch
round neck 1.5cm (⅝in) from raw
edges. Put lining on top right side
down, match centre back edges
and shoulder seams and pin at
those points. Tack lining to dress
round neck edge. Turn bodice so
that the inside of the dress is
uppermost and machine round the
neck on top of the previous row
or a fraction lower to attach collar
and lining. Remove all tackings,
trim the raw edges and snip
frequently. Turn bodice so that
dress and lining are right side out
and pull collar to extend. Holding
collar away from dress, roll the

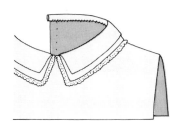

neck join between your fingers and smooth both layers of fabric away from the collar. Tack close to the neck seam, then baste lining to bodice along shoulders, round armholes, down side seams and beside centre back edges. Press neck seam with toe of iron.

CUFFS

The gathered sleeve made at the full length of the pattern can have a narrow straight cuff attached. Select any of the sleeve openings for this cuff.

The same pattern is used with the deep shaped cuff but the sleeve is cut shorter. The cuff has an overlap of 1cm (⅜in) and the horizontal opening should be used with it.

Both styles of sleeve require careful fitting. Interface the cuffs, then tack only one to the sleeve in order to fit it before stitching in place. Check the length with the arm bent so that you can see clearly how the sleeve will look in the wedding pictures. The sleeve can be shortened at the lower edge by up to 2.5cm (1in). More than this should be taken off at the sleeve head. To do this remove the tacking stitches, put one sleeve on top of the other, wrong sides together, replace the pattern with the underarm below the edge of the fabric and re-cut the whole sleeve head.

Remember to check the amount of fullness in the sleeve if it is shortened and keep it in proportion for anyone short or plump.

Narrow cuff

No pattern is provided; Fold-a-Band is used instead. Cut two pieces of lightweight Fold-a-Band 22.5cm (8¾in) long and press them to the wrong side of the fabric lining up the perforations with the straight grain – or for a special effect on some fabrics, on the bias. Press in place with a medium-hot iron and damp cloth. If the fabric you are using is unsuitable for Fold-a-Band, press it to lining instead, then baste the pieces to the wrong side of pieces of the dress fabric.

Cut out the cuffs, adding a seam allowance along each long edge of the Fold-a-Band. Fold over each end of each cuff 1cm (⅜in) on to the wrong side and press. Insert a gathering thread round the lower edge of the sleeves. Place sleeves right side out and side by side and identify which is the right sleeve and which the left. This can be discovered by looking at the sleeve head where one edge (the back) extends beyond the other. With right sides together and edges level pin one edge of the cuff to the sleeve. On the front of the sleeve the finished edge of the cuff will be level with the edge of the sleeve opening. On the back of the sleeve allow the cuff to extend beyond the opening by 1cm (⅜in). Pin the cuff ends to the sleeve, aligning the folds with the edge of the opening; pull up the gathering thread until the sleeve fits the cuff. Even out the gathers and pin together (above right). Tack cuff to sleeve, holding it

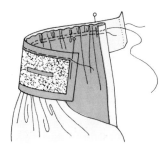

with the cuff uppermost and stitching along close beside the edge of the Fold-a-Band. Turn the sleeve over and machine stitch with gathers uppermost but following the tacking stitches. Stitch to the edge of the sleeve opening but keep the cuff ends extended and not folded under.

Remove any tacking stitches and gathering thread. Trim the raw edges and fold cuff over to extend beyond the edge of the sleeve. With the seam allowances facing into the cuff, tack just below the cuff seam, through cuff and seam allowances. Turn in cuff ends and remaining long end of cuff on to wrong side, tack and press the edges. Fold cuff along

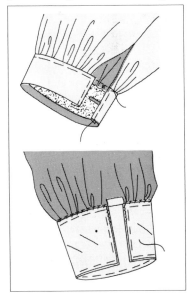

Fold-a-Band perforations and tack across each end with edges level, tacking the long fold to cover the gathered edge. Slip-stitch the cuff ends together, hem into the machine stitches along the cuff. Remove all tacking stitches. Press (see previous page).

Fasten the cuff with a button and thread or rouleau loop; the latter can be inserted in one end of the cuff before it is tacked and slip-stitched. Alternatively use a press stud or one Velcro Spot-On to fasten, or a button and buttonhole.

Deep cuff

Baste or press interfacing to wrong sides of two cuff pieces. Loops should be attached now, see p. 26. Place each one right sides together with a second cuff piece with edges level and tack along wrist edge and along sides. Stitch side edges to within 4cm (1½in) of the upper edge; stitch lower edge. Trim raw edges, cut off bottom corners, snip wrist edge turnings (below) and turn cuff right side out. Ease out the corners neatly, tack outer edge and press.

Attach cuff to sleeve, placing interfaced cuff to right side of sleeve, with edges level and cuff ends level with edge of opening when *seam allowances are extended* beyond the opening. Pull up gathers to fit, adjust and tack cuff to sleeve. Tack from cuff side, taking an even 1.5cm (⅝in) seam

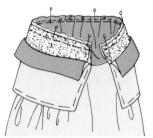

allowance, but machine the seam with gathers uppermost in order to control the gathers (above). Tack from right side of sleeve through cuff and seam allowances 5mm (¼in) below the seam line. Trim away all surplus raw edges up to the tacking. Baste round cuff through both layers to hold flat. On the inside of the cuff carefully trim 5mm (¼in) from the upper edge of remaining cuff edge, turn under cuff edge and tack with the fold level with the machine stitching. At the cuff ends turn in edges neatly, keeping the join slightly to the inside of the cuff, out of sight. Press, then complete by hemming along cuff into machine stitching and slip-stitch the ends. Remove all tackings.

CUTTING OUT AND MARKING

Having decided which features to combine in one dress, add together the amounts of fabric required from the chart on p. 112. These quantities do not of course allow for possible dovetailing of pieces, nor can they allow for more than one dress being made from the same fabric when they also could be dovetailed, possibly saving some material. You will need plenty of spare fabric for experimenting and to allow for changes of mind, but if you are very experienced and wish to

economize, prepare all pattern pieces and lay them out at home on a cutting board (if you have one) or on a sheet; then measure off the amount of fabric required.

Having prepared all pattern pieces and adjusted them to length, begin by measuring off the amount required for the skirt. Each panel takes the full width of the fabric if it is 90cm (36in) or 115cm (45in) wide, so for a four-panelled skirt cut off and put aside four skirt lengths; for six panels cut off six lengths and so on, and the same for the train. Next mark off and cut the amount needed for skirt frills. Count up the number of widths of material required and cut each one across the fabric to the depth given. Put these aside. Now cut out the sleeves. The fitted sleeve pattern is pinned to fabric folded double; make sure the straight grain is correct, place the sleeve as close as possible to the selvedges to leave a straight strip along the fold that could be opened out and used for bias strips. The full sleeve is cut from two widths of fabric placed one on top of the other wrong sides together. Pin the pattern close to one selvedge, match the straight grain line and cut out. Finally, fold the remaining fabric and pin the bodice pattern pieces in position, with grain lines correctly placed and edges marked 'fold' to the fold of the fabric and following the appropriate layout below. Work out where you will cut the other items such as cuffs and facings, but cut out only the part of the dress you intend to work on first so that you can make a start on construction. Cut out other pieces as you require them, but do not leave pins in the fabric meanwhile.

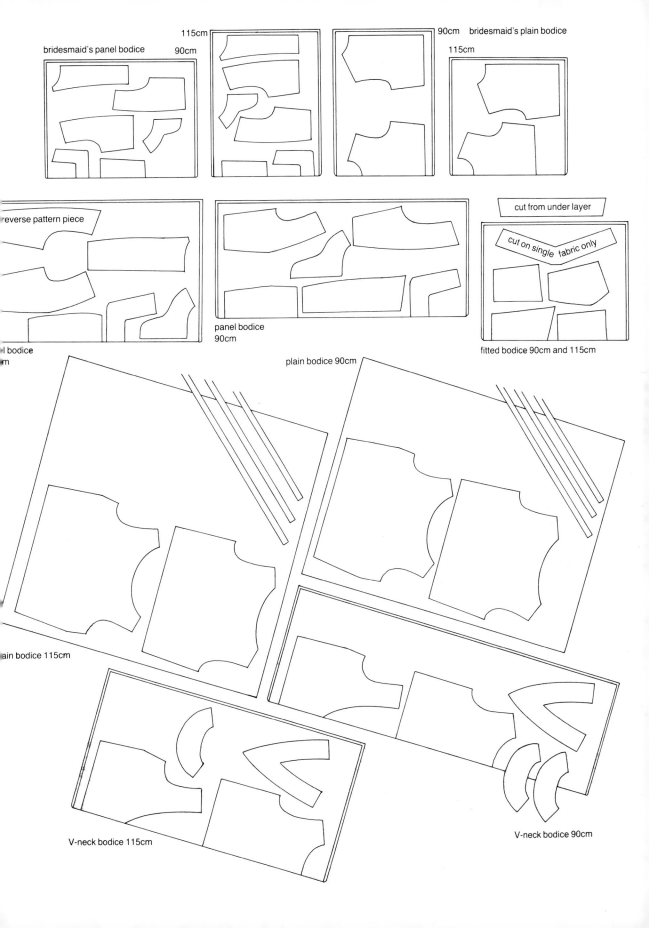

bridesmaid's panel bodice

115cm

90cm

90cm   bridesmaid's plain bodice

115cm

reverse pattern piece

cut from under layer

cut on single fabric only

l bodice
m

panel bodice
90cm

fitted bodice 90cm and 115cm

plain bodice 90cm

ain bodice 115cm

V-neck bodice 115cm

V-neck bodice 90cm

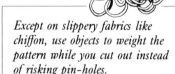

Marking the fabric

In general, avoid traditional tailor tacks; removing them can harm the fabric. Try alternatives. For example, use a fabric marker pen: some need an application of water to remove the mark, so try it out on the fabric first; others disappear automatically. Use short pieces of basting tape, except on the right side of velvet and other fabrics with delicate right side. Tailor's chalk will show up on many fabrics as a dull line, but another alternative is a sliver of soap which melts away when you press. Balance marks at the edges of the fabric can be indicated by *tiny* snips at the edge. Pins too can be used at specific points, provided they are left in for only a short time. Pierce the fabric with the point, pushing it right in up to the head. *Never* use dressmaker's carbon paper on wedding fabrics. *Never* use coloured tailor's chalk.

DARTS

Mark dart on wrong side of fabric; fold dart right side inside and match the marks. Tack from wide end to a point. Put darts side

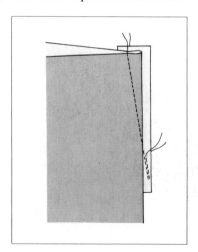

by side and mark the ends so that they are the same length. In opaque fabrics cut two pieces of lining fabric 1cm (⅜in) longer than the darts and 1cm (⅜in) wide. Put the strip under the dart and stitch through it as you sew the dart. Sew beyond the point onto the strip (below left). Reverse the stitching at the end. Remove tackings, press dart stitching, press dart down towards waist. The strip prevents the dart from caving in and eliminates wrinkled stitching.

On transparent fabrics, stitch the dart, trim off folded edge to 3–4mm (⅛in) and using the machine thread ends oversew to neaten. Press dart down towards waist.

ELASTIC

Use in sleeves, petticoat, neckline flounce etc. Elastic webbing is less bulky than conventional core elastic and does not curl over. Decide on a suitable width, measure carefully on the body allowing 2cm (¾in) for joining. It is as uncomfortable to have elastic too loose as too tight. Measure round the waist fairly closely, measure top arms and elbow positions firmly and measure wrists (where there will be no movement) tightly. If you are not sure of the exact tightness, pin the length of elastic on the wearer at the start of the fitting session and by the end of the time she will be able to say if it feels uncomfortably tight. Also, when using a casing, join elastic by stitching across with the ends extended; then if it needs altering at the last minute, all you have to do is re-stitch. Complete garment as far as possible, attach lace etc. and press.

Except on slippery fabrics like chiffon, use objects to weight the pattern while you cut out instead of risking pin-holes.

Attaching directly to fabric

With this method, up to one and a half times the length of the elastic can be pulled up. Mark the position for placing one edge of the elastic, using a row of dots on the wrong side of the fabric. Divide into quarters and mark. Measure and cut the elastic, join the ends if it is to be attached to a circle of fabric, i.e. sleeve. Mark into quarters. Place elastic on wrong side of fabric, matching one pair of marks; set stitch to zig-zag or running zig-zag and start with a few stitches, reversing to anchor the threads. Stitch forward, stretching the elastic and bringing the next pair of marks together. With narrow elastic work one row of stitching down the centre, but if it is more than 1.5cm (⅝in) wide, stitch along both edges, keeping the fabric flat for the second row.

Elastic in flat casing

With this method any amount of fabric can be gathered up. The casing is applied to the back of the fabric.

Cut a length of bias fabric or lining the width of the elastic plus 1cm (⅜in), plus an allowance for the thickness of the elastic. Alternatively, use bias binding pressed flat or knitted binding, if the width is suitable. Neaten the long edges if using fabric. Mark the position of one edge of the casing on the wrong side of the garment. Turn under one end of casing strip, place it at a garment seam on the wrong side and stitch 1cm (⅜in) from the edge. A small zig-zag stitch looks attractive, but allowance has to be made for the width of it. At the far end, turn in the end of the strip so that the two folds meet. If the casing is wide, insert a row of basting down the centre to hold it flat. Work the second row of stitching within the other edge, checking its position by measuring from the first row the width of the elastic *plus the thickness*.

Elastic in self casing

Use this method at the garment edge, e.g. petticoat waist. Cut the garment with a sufficient extension to form a casing; this should be the width of the elastic, plus a little ease, plus an allowance for the thickness, plus 1.5cm (⅝in) seam allowance. Neaten the edge of the garment. Fold the edge on to the wrong side by the amount calculated and press. Machine with straight or small zig-zag stitch just above the neatened edge. Leave a gap 1cm (⅜in) long and fasten off.

Thread elastic, keeping it flat by pinning across it at intervals as it is pulled through. Join the ends. Do not stitch up the gap in case it needs altering.

Shirring

The secrets of using single core elastic thread successfully are to wind the elastic on to the machine bobbin under tension, i.e. using the normal thread-winding mechanism, and to keep an open mind about how many rows you will make. The third tip – to hold the finished shirring in the steam from boiling water – cannot be used on all fabrics. Do not try it on silk; test all other materials by

taking a small sample.

Stitch through a single layer of fabric only. To shirr an entire section such as the bodice panel, stitch a piece of fabric and then cut out the panel. To elasticate sleeves at the wrist, shirr the sleeve before stitching the main seam. Put the bobbin filled with elastic in the machine, thread the top with synthetic thread such as Drima for strength. Set the stitch to a long straight stitch or running zig-zag. You can work a few stitches on a scrap of fabric to look at the effect, but do not expect it to look very much gathered.

Mark the position of the first row with dots made with a fabric pen. Stitch with fabric right side up. The second and subsequent rows must be parallel and the fabric must be flattened. For close spacing, use the foot as a guide in keeping straight. For wider spacing, either mark all rows with fabric pen or attach a quilting bar to the machine foot. If you are shirring fabric to fit as on a sleeve, keep adding rows until it is sufficiently tight. Anchor the ends of elastic by tying knots on the wrong side using the thread, then make sure the seam stitching crosses the lines of elastic. Further reinforcement can be made by stitching a piece of tape or knitted binding to the wrong side of the fabric to cover all the ends of the rows. Rows of shirring can be used as decorative gathering at the waist of a skirt below the bodice to give a ruched effect and also over the top of gathered sleeves. Use one row of shirring to gather up long frills and flounces when the amount of gathering does not have to be calculated precisely.

FACINGS

Square and sweetheart necks

The necklines of the panel bodice, both adult and childrens' sizes, are finished with a facing on the inside. The facing pieces can be cut from lining material if the dress fabric is bulky.

Insert the zip in the centre back seam or attach rouleau loops for buttoned fastening. With bodice right side out, place front facing in position right side down with neck edges level. Tack, starting and finishing 5cm (2in) below the shoulder seam. Place back facings in position right side down with neck edges level and centre back edges level. Pin in position. Place bodice on the pressing surface right side up and press back the shoulder edges of the facing so that when creased they meet over the dress shoulder seam. Lift the facing clear of the dress and stitch the seams. Trim the edges. Tack the remainder of the facing to the neck up to the shoulders and round the back neck. Neaten the outer edge of the facing (below).

If the bodice has a neckline zip, the facing should lie on top and the stitching will pass across the

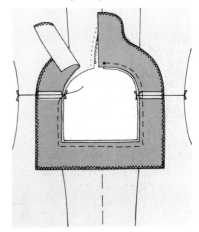

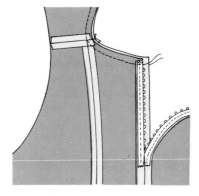

top of the zip to the edge of the seam allowance. The stitching that attaches the facing must stop at the corners at the top of the zip (above).

If the bodice is to have a button fastening, tack the neck facing to bodice down centre back edges to the dot marked on the pattern. The stitching that attaches the facing will extend down the back edges as far as the dot. With bodice uppermost, check that you have an accurate line on which to stitch, marking one if necessary with fabric pen. The important points to mark are the corners of the square neck, corners and centre front of the sweetheart neck and the two corners at the back at the top of the opening or zip (below). Stitch facing to neckline, working with bodice uppermost in order to follow the seam

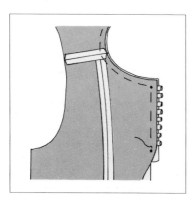

line. Swivel at corners, leaving the needle down in the fabric. Make the machine stitch smaller and stitch again 2cm (¾in) on each side of the front corners of the neck. This will reinforce the corners and reduce fraying. If the fabric frays badly, press a small piece of Bondaweb over the corner on top of the stitching; this will melt and fuse the fabric layers when the neckline is pressed.

Remove tacking stitches. Press the stitching, trim the seam allowances and snip the shaped edges of the neckline. Snip right up to the stitching at the corners and at the centre of the sweetheart neck. Cut off the corners at the back neck. Turn facing to inside of bodice, roll the seam at the edge until it is slightly inside the bodice, tack round the neck edge. Press lightly.

Baste round neckline 5cm (2in) from the edge to hold facing in position. If the fabric is firm try putting several pieces of Wundaweb between interfacing and the bodice; press carefully and the facing will remain in position. Alternatively decorative top stitching could be added on the centre back edge of the facing alongside the zip teeth. Work a bar tack to hold facing edges together below zip or loops (above right).

Catch the facings to the bodice at the shoulder and panel seams by hemming along the edge of the facing.

If lace edging, piping or other decoration is required it should be attached to the neck edge of the bodice on the seam line before the facing is attached.

Avoid pressing the neck edge from the right side unless it is covered with a dry cloth to

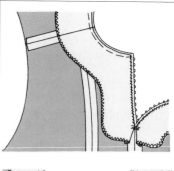

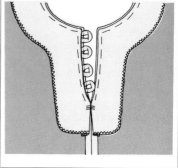

prevent causing an imprint of the facing and seams.

V Neck Bodice

The deep V neck is finished with a double band of fabric which can be matching or contrast fabric. If you wish to add decoration, attach interfacing to the wrong side of an area of fabric, mark out the shape of the band, work the decoration and then cut out the pieces.

You will need a front and back outer band and a front and back inner band. The inner band can be cut from lining fabric if the dress fabric is bulky. Mark the centre front and centre back positions. Cut out the main front and back bodice pieces but it helps prevent stretching if you cut a higher front neckline, trimming it only after the outer band has been attached. Mark centre back and centre front on bodice and also mark the neckline.

It is difficult to achieve a good finish on a shaped inset band by stitching with right sides together, a much easier method of attaching it is as follows:

After cutting out all pieces of fabric, trim 1.5cm (⅝in) from the outer edge of the front and back band pattern pieces. Use them to cut interfacing and press or baste it to the wrong side of the outer bands. Join the bodice shoulder seams, the shoulders of the outer neck band and the shoulders of the inner neckband. Neaten the outer edge of the inner neckband. Trim the outer edge of the outer neckband so that it extends no more than 1cm (⅜in) beyond the interfacing. Snip the fabric edge almost to the interfacing all round. With right side up fold the edge of the neckband over the interfacing and tack near the fold.

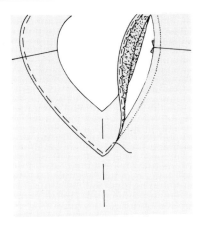

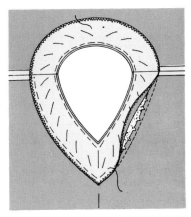

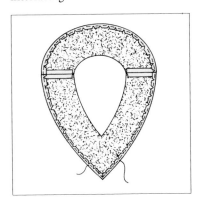

At the point tack round a second time to hold the edges flat in a neat shape (above). If you wish to check the accuracy of the shape replace the paper pattern. Press the tacked edge lightly.

Place neckband on the right side of bodice, matching centre back, centre front and shoulder seams. Tack in place. Attach band either by machining on the tacked edge with a small straight or decorative stitch or, invisibly, by working small hand catch stitching just under the edge (above).

Place inner band to bodice right sides together. Match centre back, centre front and shoulder seams. Tack and stitch round the neckline first, making sure the band is an even width by marking a stitching line with a row of dots using a fabric pen. Trim and snip the neck turnings, roll the inner band to the inside of the bodice. Roll the edge so that the seam cannot be seen from the outside and tack the edge. Hold inner band flat inside bodice and baste round the neck through both bands. Tack neatened edge of band flat on top of snipped seam allowance of bodice (above right). Attach by working back stitch by hand through band and into seam allowance underneath, taking shallow stitches to ensure that the outer bodice is not penetrated.

If you prefer to machine the neckband in place the stitching attaching the outer band could be left until the inner band is in place and then one row of machine stitching only would be added at the end through all layers. Remove all tacking stitches and press the bodice.

If you have to cut a pattern piece several times, such as the skirt panels, or if pieces like sleeves have to be cut on a single fabric, it is worth making copies of the pattern. You can then lay out every piece you need before cutting anything, thus eliminating any chance of possible error, such as two sleeves for the same arm.

FRILLS AND RUFFLES

These can be any width, either straight or shaped and made from any fabric. Finish the outer edge before attaching. Two layers of different widths gathered together will produce a luxurious effect. If the frill is not of a precise predetermined length, the gathering up can be done with shirring elastic so that the frill is stretched to fit the garment rather than pulled up. See drawing overleaf.

In general the length of frill will need to be twice the length of the garment edge, with more for fine fabrics like voile and chiffon; three times the amount for smocking and never less than one

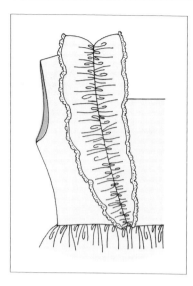

and a half times even for a deep hemline frill. If you are having the fabric permanently pleated, allow the amount required for the particular style of pleating.

Straight frills – single fabric

Cut all pieces on the straight grain to the depth required, plus 1.5cm ($\frac{5}{8}$in) at the gathered edge and 1.5–2cm ($\frac{5}{8}$–$\frac{3}{4}$in) for a narrow hem at the other edge, or 3cm (1$\frac{1}{4}$in) if the fabric is firm and you intend using Wundaweb in the hem. Join frill pieces end to end with French or narrow seams. Finish the hem and add any decoration such as ribbon, lace etc. Insert gathering threads along the upper edge, between the seams. If the frill is to be attached to the dress hem, make sure the length is correct by pinning a short section to the dress and measuring the total length. Adjust the position of the gathering thread if necessary. Fold frill in four and press creases at the edges; mark the quarters. Divide into eight if the frill is long. If the frill is very full, pull up the

gathering threads to make it a more manageable size.

There are two ways of completing the next stage. The easiest one is to leave open one garment seam, attach the frill, then stitch the seam from frill edge right through garment; the fabric can be laid flat on the table for this method and the gathering more easily arranged, but the seam must be of the type that is inconspicuous or that is decorated afterwards – e.g. centre back seam of dress, covered later with lace ruffles, ribbon bows, train etc. The second method is to stitch all the garment seams, join the final seam on the frill and then attach one to the other. Decide which method is appropriate and also whether to attach the frill with an overlaid seam which is the easiest method – the stitching can be

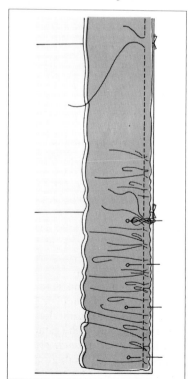

covered with ribbon etc. or you can use a machine embroidery stitch – or to join in the usual way with right sides together.

For both methods divide garment into four or eight, pin frill to garment matching all the marks, pull up the gathering thread in one section only and wind ends round a pin to anchor. Even out the gathers, inserting pins across the seam. Tack the section and fasten off (below). Remove pins. Move to the next section, pin and tack. If using an overlaid seam, stitch on the right side on the edge, using a straight or zig-zag stitch. On the wrong side, remove the gathering threads, trim and neaten the edges.

If frill and garment are right sides together, stitch with frill uppermost, feeding the gathers under the foot carefully and stitching a fraction below the tacking. Remove the gathering threads, trim and neaten the edges or make self-finish seam. Note that for heavy, deep hemline frills you can pin and then machine baste for strength instead of hand tacking.

Straight ruffles

For long narrow ruffles attached to the right side, cut pieces of fabric allowing for a narrow hem on each edge. Join the pieces. Finish the hems and attach lace etc. Insert a gathering thread down the middle of the ruffle. Fold into four and mark. Complete garment edges or seams and divide into four the area where the ruffle is to go. Pin end of ruffle to garment. Put under the machine foot and stitch for 1cm ($\frac{3}{8}$in), removing the pin. Pin the next ruffle point to the corresponding point on the garment,

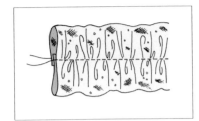

pull up the gathers, even them out and stitch, carefully feeding in the gathers and controlling them. Remove the pin, gather up next section and so on. Use this method for lace ruffles too.

If the ruffles are short or the fabric is difficult to handle, you may prefer to pin and tack before stitching. Apply ribbon, beads etc. to the middle of the ruffle if you wish.

An alternative method for fine fabrics such as net, voile and chiffon is to cut strips of fabric just over twice the required finished width, fold in each edge to overlap at the middle, press and insert a gathering thread down the centre which goes through all three layers (above).

Double frill – straight

Cut strips of fabric twice the required finished length plus two seam allowances. Join the pieces, fold wrong side inside and press. Baste together if fabric is slippery. Insert gathering thread and attach as described for single frills.

When hand-sewing, sit on your bed supported by pillows and with the dress spread out around you. This keeps crushing to the minimum and the bed supports the weight of the dress.

Double frill – shaped

Cut two pieces for each frill, place right sides together and stitch outer edge (below left). Trim, snip and turn right side out. Roll the join to the edge and press, or tack and press. Insert a gathering thread in the raw edge (below right). Attach as described for single frills, or in the case of short frills in the bodice seams; stitch the frill to one bodice section, place the second section on top right side down, stitch again and turn right side out.

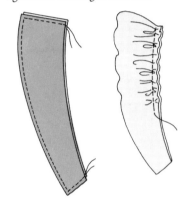

Single fluted frills

These are applied to the right side and stitched to produce a narrow fluted upper edge. Complete the garment hem. Cut and join the pieces of fabric. Turn a hem at the lower edge and attach lace etc. Make a narrow decorative hem at the upper edge, e.g. shell edge or zig-zag. On non-fraying taffeta, several layers can be used and all edges pinked. Insert a gathering thread 2–3cm (¾–1¼in) inside the upper edge, divide frill into four or eight and apply to the right side of the garment, stitching over the gathering thread with a small zig-zag stitch. Do not remove the gathering thread. This type of frill can be

attached so that the lower edge is either level with the garment hem or above it (above).

HEMS

The hem of a long or a short dress can be marked, turned up and tacked at any stage after the shoulders and waist have been fitted. In fact, with a long dress you will be glad to get the surplus material up out of the way for the fittings, but it is advisable to leave the actual stitching to the end.

Plain hemlines: marking the length

LONG DRESS   Select one of the following methods:

With the bride standing at the top of the stairs and you sitting a couple of steps below, mark the hem 2.5cm (1in) from the floor. It is more convenient to use a simple block of wood than a hem-marker. Mark a line along the wood 2.5cm (1in) up and put it just under the edge of the skirt. You can of course use it for the petticoats too, marking several

If the dress hangs limply, add more to the petticoat in the form of frills where needed rather than trying to stiffen the dress.

VARIATION ON DRESS NO. 1
Soft, flowing long-sleeved dress with integral train and long streaming veil. The centre of the panel bodice may be smocked, ruched or shirred. The shaped cuffs are fastened with loops and buttons and seamed to the full sleeves with picot-edged taffeta frills. Work the picot edge by machine, or hand roll the hems and sew tiny pearls in place as you stitch, or attach picot-edge ribbon. Repeat the finish on waist frill, hem frill and on the edge of the veil

lines at the correct height on the wood. Insert pins in the fabric at intervals of about 30cm (12in). The bride must be sure to turn slowly and to stand as erect as she will at the wedding. Having worked round once, fluff out the dress so that the skirt falls in a different position and go round again putting pins along the newly exposed sections.

Another method is to mark a level line at about mid-calf where the fabric hangs smoothly, note exactly how much longer the dress is to be, then add that amount with the garment flat on the table.

SHORT DRESS   Use a hem-marker or improvise by attaching a long ruler or a length of wood to a wood block. Use pins rather than the chalk in the hem-marker in case this does not brush off easily. Turn up a short amount of hem at the front to the level required and then pin. Look at it from a distance, adjust the pins to lengthen or shorten if necessary. Put one pin in the fold of the hem, remove all the others and let the surplus fabric hang down. Work all round the skirt inserting pins at that level. To make it easier and to avoid mistakes, stick a piece of basting tape across the

hem-marker at the level you want. You may find it more comfortable to sit on the stairs to pin.

Marking hemlines: pre-finished – scallops, border designs, etc.

Tack the lining or under layer to the bodice at the waist and, before inserting the zip, mark the hemline at the required level. Place the upper layer over it and gather and tack it below the waist line, attaching it to the layer beneath. Adjust it from the waist, raising or lowering every few centimetres (inches) until the over-dress is exactly 13mm ($\frac{1}{2}$in) longer

DRESS: DESIGN NO. 1

The panelled bodice with full sleeve gathered into the deep cuff. The bodice fastens with one button at the top of the centre back seam. The skirt has six panels.

Pattern (see drawings page 121)

PIECES: 2, 3, 4, 5, 6, 7 for bodice
8(D), 10 for sleeve
1(A) for skirt

Cutting out

Cut out six skirt panels; front and back bodice panels on double fabric; neck facings to fold. Cut two sleeves and cut cuff pattern four times. Mark centres of skirt panels, mark centre front of bodice and balance marks. Cut out facings in Vilene.

Making up

1. BODICE   Attach Vilene to bodice neckline. Stitch centre back seam to dot. Stitch back panel seams (right). Stitch front panel seams, press seam allowances towards centre

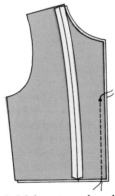

(right). Make one rouleau loop and stitch on right side of back neckline. Place loop with ends level with centre back edge 2cm ($\frac{3}{4}$in) below neck edge. Stitch front and back bodice together at shoulder seams.

2. FACINGS   Attach neck facings. See p. 33. Stitch right seam of bodice.

3. SKIRT   Join all skirt panels, leaving an opening for the zip at the top of one of them. Press all seams. Tack up hem if possible. Gather up skirt and attach to bodice. See p. 54.

4. ZIP   Insert zip in left side seam between dot in skirt seam and armhole. See p. 55.

5. SLEEVES   Make sleeve opening. See p. 45. Make rouleau loops if desired and attach four to each cuff. Make up cuffs. Attach cuffs to sleeves. See p. 29. Gather sleeve head and insert sleeves in bodice.

Sew buttons to cuffs. Attach Velcro if loops are not being used. Sew button to bodice neckline. Stitch hem. Remove all tackings from dress. Press.

all round. Get someone to help you if the dress is long. Undo the waist tacking and re-tack with the over layer included. This is not easy to do and you should be prepared to spend some time getting the hemline right.

An alternative method if the under and overskirt are the same width is to mark and finish the hem of the underdress, unpick the waist join, spread out the skirt, place the over layer on top, and starting at the hem in order to have it correctly placed, baste the two pieces together from hem to waist with several rows of tacking. Rejoin skirt to bodice.

HEMLINE WITH DEEP FINISH, e.g. FRILL, QUILTED BAND, etc.   Make upper skirt section, tack to bodice at waist, finish and insert zip if you can. Mark a line of pins round the skirt an even distance from the floor. This is a guideline for attaching the made-up band or frill. Even if the line is not at the correct level, you can mark another parallel with it. The frill or band has of course to be carefully made to an even width.

Turning up the hem

Spread out the skirt with the hem nearest to you. Check the pins and make sure they follow a reasonably smooth line. Adjust or remove any that are obviously in the wrong position. Work a row of

Before you cut out, examine the entire length of fabric for flaws and if necessary arrange your pattern pieces to ensure that any of these will not be seen. They can usually be concealed near the hem, under the arm, beneath frills, lace etc.

tacking stitches along the row of pins. Take up small amounts of fabric, but leave stitches on the surface about 5cm (2in) long. Remove the pins as you reach them. You will be able to make a smoother line if you stand up to do this, so that you can see the pins ahead and not just the one immediately in front. This line of tacking will fall on the lower edge of the dress, so turn up the hem surplus and, with the tacking on the lower edge, tack again 5mm (¼in) from the fold. If you wish to check the level once more, tack a second time above that, to hold the surplus against the dress; then try it on to check. When you are satisfied, press the fold lightly, then finish the hem in a way that is suitable for the fabric. If you select a method that is new to you, make a sample first.

Skirt lengths

LONG DRESS   The dress or overdress should clear the ground by 2.5cm (1in) when the bride or bridesmaid is standing still and wearing her shoes and petticoats. All layers beneath the dress should each in turn be 13mm (½in) shorter. So, if the dress is an overdress on top of an underdress and beneath is the lining and one petticoat, the measurements are as follows:

PETTICOAT   7cm (2½in) from ground. Lining: 5 cm (2in) from ground. Underdress: 4cm (1½in) from ground. Overdress: 2.5cm (1in) from ground.

It is easier if you turn up and finish the petticoat hems and any other layers not attached to the dress when you are making them rather than leaving them all until the end. If you are not making all

the long dresses, ensure that the other dressmakers have the above information.

SHORT DRESS   The bride can decide on the length she wants and should then give directions to the bridesmaids. This cannot be in the form of a measurement, but will have to be a reference on the body such as 8cm (3in) below the knee, 10cm (4in) above the ankle bone etc.; they should also be told what method of finishing the hem is required and what depth it should be. Shoes and petticoats must be worn and the various skirt layers should differ in length by the amounts given for a long dress.

Hem fullness

Few bridal fabrics can be shrunk or manoeuvred to dispose of fullness that appears in a deep shaped hem; if you insert tucks or darts they may show as ridges, so the answer is to insert a gathering thread in the hem edge. Turn up and tack the hem fold (below top). Use fine crochet yarn in a pale colour, set the machine to a

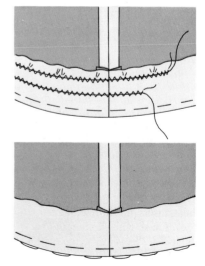

medium zig-zag and couch the yarn to the hem by zig-zagging over it. Work one row half-way between hem fold and hem edge, the other 5mm ($\frac{1}{4}$in) below the edge. Draw up the yarn gently and even out the gathers until the hem lies *almost* flat on the garment (below opposite). Do not pull it quite flat. Neaten the hem edge or work a row of straight stitching just above the yarn, holding the gathers flat. Complete the hem. Remove both gathering threads. Note that there will be no fullness in narrow hems.

Hem finishes

The following are suitable for dress hems, linings and petticoats. Select according to fabric.

Deep hems

2.5–8cm (1–3in) Suitable for fabrics that fray little and also for thick heavy fabrics.

Pinked

Mark the hem depth 1cm ($\frac{3}{8}$in) or more below the trimmed edge. Work a row of small zig-zag stitches on the line. Trim the edge with pinking shears. Tack the hem to garment and catch stitch or herringbone between the layers.

Folded and hemmed (a)

Suitable for fine or transparent fabrics. Allow the maximum amount of hem depth up to about 13cm (5in) and trim the edge level. Press the tacked fold well, then remove the tacking stiches. Tuck in the raw edge until it reaches the fold, smooth out the hem, insert pins horizontally, then tack. Finish with slip hemming. Note that this is not suitable for a very flared hemline.

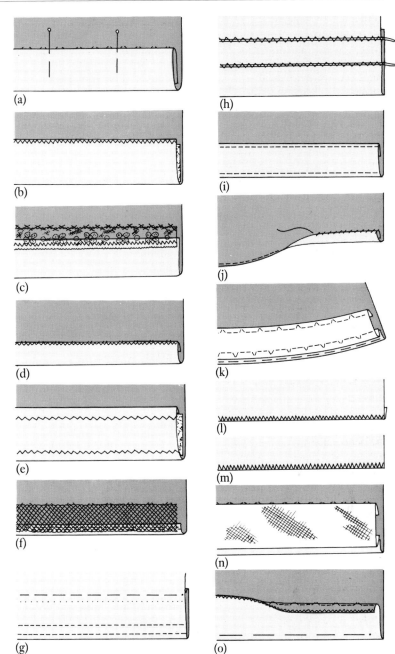

(a) (b) (c) (d) (e) (f) (g) (h) (i) (j) (k) (l) (m) (n) (o)

Wundaweb hem (b)

Suitable for firm fabrics; try it out first. Cut the hem edge with pinking shears or work a row of running zig-zag (ordinary zig-zag may cause a ridge) 2.5cm (1in) from the tacked fold. Press the hem. Remove the tackings. Place the Wundaweb under the hem with one edge at the fold; replace the hem and press with a medium–hot iron over a damp cloth, pressing sharply until the Wundaweb has melted. Make sure it has fused completely at seams where fabric is double. If a deeper hem is required make it twice the length and insert two rows of Wundaweb. Make sure they touch or else bubbling may occur.

Stretch lace finish hem (c)

Suitable for medium or heavy fabrics that fray. Trim hem edge level, stitch one side of lace 1cm (⅜in) below edge, using a small zig-zag stitch. Tack lace to garment. Finish by hemming or herringboning along the other edge. Alternatively, leave tacked if stitching is to be added to the right side, e.g. top stitching, ribbon trim. Make sure the stitching holds the lace in position. Another method of finishing the lace involves trimming the hem edge to 5mm (¼in) after stitching the lace in position; then use the lace to bind the edge, holding down the second edge by working a large half back-stitch from the

If seams on plain fabrics wrinkle, especially near the hem, try putting Wundaweb under the seam allowances, but try it on a sample of the fabric first to make sure it is not visible. Cut Wundaweb into narrow strips. Place the seam wrong side up on the ironing board and stretch it, pinning it to the board at both ends. Slip the Wundaweb beneath the seam allowances and press, using a damp muslin cloth, until the Wundaweb has properly melted. Do not move the seam until cold.

right side, right round the hem. Finish the hem by slip-hemming the fold of the lace to the garment.

Stitched edge hem (d)

Suitable for lightweight but not transparent fabrics. Turn under and press the hem edge no less than 5mm (¼in) deep. Work a small zig-zag over the edge. Turn up hem and tack to garment. Finish with catch stitch under the edge, picking up the zig-zag thread rather than fabric.

Stiffened hem (e)

Suitable for medium to heavy fabrics, this uses iron-on Vilene. Test the Vilene on the fabric and select a grade that is suitable. Turn up and tack and press the hemline in the usual way. Trim to 4cm (1½in). Remove the tacking stitches and insert strips of Vilene 6–9cm (2½–3½in) wide and with one edge shaped to fit the lower edge of hem. Have the adhesive *towards* the dress. Tack or pin hem edge to Vilene. Work two rows of zig-zag or running zig-zag through hem and Vilene, one near the bottom and the other close to the edge. Carefully replace hem edge in position against dress and press so that Vilene adheres to dress.

Horsehair braid (f)

Use polypropylene stiffening (horsehair braid). Turn up, tack and press hem. Trim to 2cm (¾in) and attach to dress either with catch stitch or one or two rows of machine stitching. Tack the braid on top with lower edge 2mm (1/16in) above lower edge of hem. Catch stitch each edge to hem. To join the ends of the stiffening, trim them so that the edges meet

and then cover the join by hemming a piece of lining or binding over the top.

Corded hem (h)

This is a machine stitched decorative hem suitable for medium and heavy fabrics. Select a round thread to be couched on to the fabric such as crochet cotton. The same hem finish can be used on sleeve hems and also to decorate the front and back bodice panels. Mark and turn up the hem, tack and press the fold. Turn the hem edge to a suitable depth, neaten it and tack it flat to the dress. Mark a line on the outside 5mm (¼in) below the level of the hem edge. Set the machine stitch to a zig-zag wide enough to cover the yarn you have chosen. Attach the quilting foot with short toes. Begin 5cm (2in) beyond a skirt seam, lay the yarn on the fabric, slide the fabric under the foot, lower the foot and stitch, feeding the yarn under the centre of the foot. On completion, stop before reaching the end; leave the foot down, but carefully snip the stitching in the seam in front of the foot. Trim both ends of yarn and push them through the hole to the wrong side. Complete the zig-zag. Stitch as many rows as you wish, spacing them to look right on the fabric.

Top-stitched hem (g)

Suitable for all fabrics except those liable to wrinkle. Make a trial sample, sewing two rows of straight, zig-zag or wide-spaced twin needle stitching close to the fold and two more some distance away. This distance will depend on how much hem there is to turn up and also on the effect created on the fabric, but try to have the hem at least 5cm (2in) deep. On the dress trim the hem edge level; zig-zag the edge. Tack hem to garment. From the right side, work the row of stitching above the hem fold, remove the tacking on the fold, then stitch on the fold. Using an adjustable marker, measure the distance you want between the rows and mark a row of dots on the fabric.

Stitch on the dots, remove tackings, stitch for the final time.

Blind-hemstitched hem (o)

Suitable for medium and heavy fabrics. Neaten or pink the hem edge at a suitable depth. Tack hem to garment 2cm ($\frac{3}{4}$in) below the edge. Attach blind hemming foot to machine, adjust stitch, fold hem back on to the right side, allowing 5mm ($\frac{1}{4}$in) of hem edge to extend. Stitch, making sure that the needle only just catches the fabric when it swings to the left.

Net hem (n)

Suitable for lace fabrics. Use soft net or veiling. Mark hemline on lace; do not turn up, instead attach a 5cm (2in) wide strip of net to right side of lace, sewing on the hemline itself. Trim lace to the minimum. Turn under and tack the other edge of the net. Finish by slip-hemming net to lace. Note stretch lace can be used instead of net.

Alternatively if you want the lace folded up as the hem – and this is perfectly acceptable provided you can match or almost match the design – tack in the usual way, but trim all round the hem following the outline of the design, then stitch to garment by working wide-spaced loopstitch over the edge.

NARROW HEMS 2mm–1.5cm ($\frac{1}{16}$–$\frac{5}{8}$in)

Fine-line hem (m)

Suitable for all transparent fabrics or jersey; can also be used on medium weight fabrics to produce a picot edge. Cut hem to exact length required. Set machine to a very small zig-zag. Place tissue paper under the edge to prevent it curling over; stitch evenly over the raw edge from right side.

Zig-zag hem (l)

Suitable for transparent fabrics. Cut hem to length plus 5mm ($\frac{1}{4}$in). Set machine to fairly small zig-zag. Put hem under machine foot right side up, fold edge under 5mm ($\frac{1}{4}$in) and stitch over the edge. Using small scissors, trim away any surplus fabric close to the stitching.

Faced hem (k)

Suitable for medium weight fabrics. Turn up and tack hem on the fold. Press, trim the edge to 1cm ($\frac{3}{8}$in). Tack bias binding (purchased or made from lining fabric) over the hem with one edge almost level with the hem edge. Turn right side up and machine with two rows of decorative stitching. Alternatively, use stretch lace instead of binding.

Rolled hem (j)

Suitable for all fine fabrics. By machine, cut to length plus 1cm ($\frac{3}{8}$in). Attach hemming foot to machine, set stitch. Trim fabric edge cleanly and feed through foot wrong side up. By hand, work a row of straight stitching 3mm ($\frac{1}{8}$in) from the marked hemline. Trim fabric close to stitching. Use short pieces of thread and roll and hem the edge.

Complete frill edges before gathering and attaching to the dress. Choose from narrow stitched hems, shell edge, binding, Wundaweb, lace. If there are lots of frills on the design you choose, or if you have several bridesmaids to dress, get out the hemming foot and shell hemming foot that go with your machine, or buy these if you have not already got them. Practise on spare fabric until you have the knack of controlling it, then use the foot wherever you can, including round the edge of the veil.

Moisten your fingers to grip the fabric and roll it as finely as possible.

Remember – try to do as much pressing as possible before final stitching. Try not to press over the finished hem but if you have to do so, slide a folded piece of fabric against the hem edge to level up the layers. Cover the right side with dry pressing cloth.

Flat hem (i)

Suitable for all fabrics. Practise on a spare piece of material to find the narrowest width of hem possible on the fabric. It should be 5mm–1.5cm ($\frac{1}{4}$in–$\frac{5}{8}$in). On thin or fraying fabrics, turn under the raw edge, tack to garment, press. Machine stitch twice, once close to the bottom edge, again along the tacked edge. On thicker fabrics, zig-zag the raw edge, tack it to the garment. Machine stitch once on the fold and again below the zig-zag.

Note: You can omit the row of stitching on the fold if you prefer.

INTERFACING

Selected areas of the dresses will require interfacing in order to produce the required effect – not so that they will withstand wear, which is the customary reason for using interfacing. The choice of interfacing will depend as usual on the type of fabric being used, but aim to produce a crisper more structured result than is the case with clothes for normal wear. The fabric glossary makes recommendations for interfacing, but here are some suggestions as to where it can be used to good effect on wedding clothes. However, the success of these suggestions depends on the fabric used, so try out the interfacing on a piece of spare fabric before starting the process on the dress.

Sleeves

● Soft sew-in or iron-on Vilene attached to *both* pieces of deep cuffs, or soft sew-in Vilene for the outer cuff piece and stiffer iron-on Vilene on the inner cuff piece.
● Mount the entire sleeve onto iron-on or sew-in Vilene.
● Insert Fold-a-Band in hems of sleeves that have elastic above the edge.
● Attach sew-in or iron-on Vilene to the entire wrist edge and opening area of the fitted sleeve.

Bodice

● Mount the entire bodice on to Vilene.
● Mount centre front and centre back panels on to Vilene.

Skirt

● Mount skirt panels on to Vilene.
● Make a Vilene underskirt

attached to or separate from the dress at the waist.
● Attach a Vilene flounce to an underskirt, especially for styles with deep hemline frills.
● Insert a wide band of Vilene in the dress hem.
● Stitch narrow strips of sew-in Vilene in the seams to prevent wrinkled seams, or press strips of iron-on Vilene to the seam edges on the wrong side before stitching the seams.

Train

● Mount the entire train on to Vilene.
● Insert a wide band of Vilene round outer edge.
● Create a bustle effect by making a Vilene flounce to attach to the waist under the train.

Cutting Vilene

Fold the Vilene, place pattern pieces in position economically and hold in place. Mark round outer edge with dots, using fabric pen; also mark any balance marks, overlap points, pattern dots etc. Remove pattern. Cut out Vilene following dotted line. If Vilene is required narrower than pattern – for example for neck facing – cut 5mm ($\frac{1}{4}$in) inside the line on the outer edge. If there are several pieces similar in shape, write the name on each.

Sew-in Vilene

Cut out each garment piece in fabric; place fabric wrong side down on Vilene and baste all round 2cm ($\frac{3}{4}$in) from the edge. With larger pieces, baste through the middle also. Trim off any untidy edges of Vilene.

Iron-on Vilene

Arrange pieces of fabric wrong side up; arrange the Vilene pieces

adhesive side down, making sure the straight grain of the fabric will be as shown on the pattern. Hold with one pin in the centre. Press with medium–hot iron and damp muslin, removing the pin as you begin. Allow to cool. Cut out the pieces, cutting round the edge of the Vilene.

Fold-a-Band

Cut to length required, arrange on wrong side of fabric with perforations following straight grain. Press, using medium–hot iron and damp cloth. Soft cuff-weight Fold-a-Band may or may not be included in the garment seam, so it may be cut with or without seam allowances at the ends. Cut out round the outer edge, adding a seam allowance along each side and across the ends if necessary. If overlaps etc. have to be marked, replace the pattern piece or re-measure the fabric and mark with fabric pen. When stitching sew close beside the edge of the Fold-a-Band.

Wundaweb

Ensure that it is completely concealed between two layers of fabric and correctly positioned. Make sure the Wundaweb is not tight or stretched in the fabric. Press well, making several short sharp movements with a medium–hot iron and damp cloth until the web has melted. Wundaweb slightly stiffens the fabric so it is useful in frill edges.

Heavy or pelmet-weight Vilene

These should not be included with seam stitching, so either trim the seam allowance from the pattern before cutting the Vilene – making sure all fabric pieces are cut first – or cut the Vilene and trim the edges afterwards. Attach the Vilene to the wrong side of the fabric with basting stitches, or using pieces of Wundaweb, or with lengths of basting tape. Seam stitching should fall beside the edge of the Vilene.

Organdie and net

Soft or see-through fabrics can be interfaced with either of these materials. Cut out, using the pattern pieces, and baste the organdie or net to the wrong side of the pieces of garment. Net is a useful interfacing to attach to the wrong side of facings in fabrics where only very slight stiffening is required. It can also be used as the facing or hem itself on lace and embroidered net, or as a base for an entire garment section such as sleeves, frills and collars.

MOUNTING

This is a technique whereby each piece of garment is put on to a backing fabric and both are then handled as if they were a single layer. One part of the dress can be mounted to add stiffness, e.g. front bodice panel; or a whole section can be mounted for support e.g. chiffon or lace sleeves; or the entire dress can be mounted rather than lined. Use a fabric that suits the purpose; it could be lining material, cotton lawn, net, Vilene etc.

Cut the sections of garment and lift them – with pattern still attached – on to the length of mounting material. Cut out round the edge of each piece; there is no need to pin as the weight of the pattern and top fabric will keep it in place. Mark the balance marks etc., that can be seen at the edges, onto the mounting fabric. Remove

pattern pieces. Open out each piece of top fabric and spread them out on the table wrong side up. Place each corresponding piece of mounting fabric on top, wrong side down. Baste the two together, beginning with a row of stitches down the middle; add another row each side and on large sections insert even more rows, ending with a line of basting round each piece about 3cm (1¼in) from the raw edges to ensure that the basting stitches do not become caught up in seam stitching. Do not fasten off thread ends; do not pull the stiches tight; keep the fabric flat while basting. Use a number 7 or 8 needle and either tacking thread or fine machine embroidery thread in white. Never use sewing thread. Do not press except at the seams until the basting has been removed. If any stitches are in the way of pressing, snip the thread and remove.

Make up the dress. The two are handled as one; the additional layer will make the main hem easier to handle. Add neck interfacings, cuffs etc. as usual, even lining where required.

OPENINGS

Make the opening at the wrist or elbow, selecting a method that is suitable for the fabric. Where possible make openings before stitching the seams.

Dart opening

For long fitted sleeves in opaque fabrics. Mark the dart on the sleeve as shown on the pattern. Fold sleeve right sides together, stitch dart to dot. Press towards back of sleeve. Cut the dart along the fold from raw edge to end of

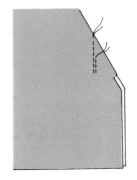

(a)

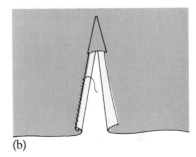

(b)

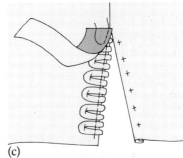

(c)

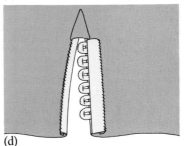

(d)

stitching then snip at an angle as shown (a). Press point of dart flat. Roll a narrow hem on the edge nearest back of sleeve. Hem (b). Decide on the method of fastening.

Fold fabric with right sides together, tack dart from sleeve edge to point. Mark base of stitching and machine dart, fastening off the thread. Press dart towards back of sleeve. Snip dart at base of stitching, then continue to cut through upper layer only to the end of the stitching. Lift upper edge to one side and finish lower layer to take the buttons. Place a narrow strip of Wundaweb under the edge of fabric and press. Alternatively, a strip of lining fabric or knitted binding can be used. Turn under the edge of the fabric and hem to sleeve or, if fabric is thick, work herringbone stitch over the edge.

On upper side of opening press a crease from stitching to sleeve edge, then remove tackings from dart. Baste or iron on a strip of Vilene to the wrong side, allowing it to extend 1.5cm ($\frac{5}{8}$in) on each side of the crease. Make a length of rouleau for the loops. Mark the button positions on the other edge, then space out loops to correspond on the other edge on the right side. Stitch loops in place. Cut a bias strip of fabric 4cm (1$\frac{1}{2}$in) wide, place it right side down on top of loops and stitch from base of dart stitching, to edge of sleeve (c). Baste edge across loops. Turn under raw edge of bias and hem to sleeve or, on thick fabrics, work herringbone

If your test seam wrinkles in satin, taffeta and other opaque fabrics, try stitching an extra strip of fabric in the seam. Use odd pieces of lining cut into 5mm ($\frac{1}{4}$in) strips on the bias. They increase the thickness of the seam and help eliminate puckers.

stitch over the edge (d). Make a bar tack at the top of the opening. The edge of the sleeve can be finished with binding or with a bias strip turned entirely to the inside of the sleeve.

Seam openings

An easy non-decorative opening suitable for all opaque fabrics where a plain seam is used. The fastening will fall at the inside of the arm, so do not use with shaped cuffs. Suitable for sleeves with bound finish. Can also be used where dense decoration, such as beading, would be interrupted by a visible opening. Stitch the sleeve seam to within 7cm (3in) of the lower edge. Press open and neaten the edges. Cut narrow strips of Wundaweb 9cm (3$\frac{1}{2}$in) long and slip them under the seam allowances. Press to bond firmly. Complete the sleeve edge as desired. Fasten inconspicuously with a press stud or flat button and thread loop.

Bound opening

Neat and visible; use on light and medium fabrics. Use self fabric or contrast texture such as satin. Cut bias strips 2cm ($\frac{3}{4}$in) wide and four times the length of the marked opening. Fold in one edge 5mm ($\frac{1}{4}$in) and press, stretching it. Cut the strip in two. If using bought binding, trim off one fold and press. Cut the opening in the sleeve. Tack the bias strip right side down to the right side of the fabric, matching raw edges at the sleeve edges. After a few stitches, allow the edge of the opening to begin to slope at an angle. Catch in a few threads of fabric at the middle of the strip. Stitch across the centre for 2cm ($\frac{3}{8}$in) or so to hold, then turn the sleeve over

and stitch right along the crease of the binding. Remove tackings. Trim raw edges a little. Press binding to extend beyond edge by pushing the toe of the iron under it on the right side. With the wrong side towards you, fold over the edge of the binding until it meets the fabric edge, then fold it again to bring it on to the machine stitching. Tack. Hem the binding down, picking up the machine stitches. Press one edge under. Attach cuffs etc. If sleeve hems are to be bound, bind the opening and hem with one continuous bias strip.

Hemmed opening

Neat; does not overlap. Use on fine and transparent fabrics where others would be too conspicuous or clumsy. Thread a small needle with a short piece of thread. Cut the opening and immediately make a rolled hem along the edge, holding it with small hemming stitches. Do not tack. Work quickly before the fabric frays. Moisten your fingers for a better grip. At the centre where there is little to turn over, fold the fabric once only and stitch right over the edge. Attach cuff etc.

Opening in lined sleeve

Use on any lined sleeve including lace lined with net, satin with chiffon over-sleeve etc. Mark the opening position on the wrong side of the lining pieces, but do not cut. Place sleeve and lining right sides together, baste round marked opening. Stitch 3mm ($\frac{1}{16}$in) on each side of the mark, sewing to a point at the bottom. Stitch again if fabric frays. Cut between the rows right to the point. Stitch the seams in the lining and in the fabric separately.

Press and turn through to bring both layers wrong sides together. Press the opening. Baste sleeve to lining along seam, round sleeve head and round the wrist. Attach cuff etc.

Horizontal opening

Quick and easy; use on full sleeves in any except transparent fabrics. Do not cut an opening; instead, make snips in the edge of the sleeve 1.5cm ($\frac{5}{8}$in) deep and 1cm ($\frac{3}{8}$in) on each side of the opening position. Fold back the 2cm ($\frac{3}{4}$in) edge, make a hem and stitch along the fold. Attach cuff with ends level with edge of opening. The opening is concealed when the cuff is fastened.

PERMANENT PLEATING

Fabrics made from man-made fibres can be permanently pleated. This includes nylon, polyester and acetate. Straight pieces of fabric, knife-pleated can be added to a hemline as deep flounces. Quarter- or half-circles can be crystal pleated and then cut to form shaped flounces on the bottom of sleeves. After pleating, cut the fabric exactly to length. Join seams on pleat folds with a tiny zig-zag stitch on the wrong side. At the hem edge zig-zag and re-press into pleats, or zig-zag and leave fluted, or stitch narrow ribbon on edge.

PIPING

Piping can be inserted in almost any seam to add emphasis and decoration. It could be used on the panel bodice seams, round the deep shaped cuffs, in the skirt seams, in seams joining frills to skirt and in the waist seam. In

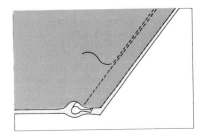

addition piping would be effective on bags, hats, round necklines and round a stiffened belt or cummerbund.

Filled piping attached to a tape can be bought by length but few of the fabrics from which they are made would be suitable for wedding clothes, with the exception of gold and silver pipings. It is easy to make piping from fabric or even from bias binding, perhaps one made from satin.

In addition to a sufficient length of bias 2.5cm (1in) wide you will need the zip foot or piping foot on the machine and some fine pre-shrunk white piping cord. Press the bias to remove some of the stretch. If using bought bias press out the folds.

With right side of bias outwards wrap it round the piping cord placing the edges flat with wrong sides together. Tack the edges together close to the cord, or hold together with basting tape. Tack the piping to the right side of one edge of the garment. Put the piping in position carefully with the filled edge extending into the garment. Tack so that the machine stitching will fall exactly on the seam line. Stitch piping to garment using the zip foot adjusted close to the cord. Place the second piece of garment on top right side down. With edges level tack through all layers. To stitch the seam turn the fabric over so that the original row of stitching is

uppermost and machine again on that stitching, still using the zip foot (opposite). Remove all tackings, trim edges and press by sliding the iron up to the piping but not over it.

Alternative decoration that can be inserted in seams in the same way include lace and other edgings, ric-rac braid and also quite simply a fold of fabric that could contrast in colour or texture with the dress.

To use fabric cut bias strips 1.5cm ($\frac{5}{8}$in) wide, press to remove some of the stretch, fold lengthways right side out and press. To insert in a seam tack and machine the strip to the right side of one piece of garment with the fold extending 3–4mm ($\frac{1}{8}$in) beyond the seam line towards the garment. Complete the seam in the same way as for the seam above.

> *Press out the central crease in the length of fabric. If any part of it is stubborn, cut out making sure you do not put it at the centre front or centre back.*

ROULEAU

Rouleau filled with piping cord can be used single or plaited as a belt and for button loops; soft rouleau is also used for loops and for ties, coils, sprays. Equip yourself with a rouleau needle if you are going to make a quantity of soft rouleau. Both types can be used as decoration, slip-stitched in lines or whirls to the outside of the garment, to bags, head-dresses etc.

Filled rouleau

Decide on the thickness you require according to your fabric and buy some piping cord; you will need plenty of cord, as each piece you make takes twice its length in cord. Work out the correct width of bias strip you need by making a sample and measuring it, allowing 1cm (⅜in) for a seam. Cut a sufficient length of bias fabric. Cut a piece of cord twice the length of the piece of fabric; wrap the fabric round the cord wrong side out, starting at the middle of the cord. With the zip foot or the piping foot on the machine, stitch across the cord close to the end of the fabric, then along to the end beside the cord (a). Turn rouleau right side out by pulling the end of the cord and pushing the fabric back over the end (b). Trim off surplus cord.

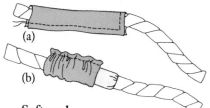

(a)

(b)

Soft rouleau

Cut strips of bias fabric 2cm (¾in) wide, press to stretch, then fold it right sides together. Stitch with a slight zig-zag stitch; have the fold of the fabric to the right and keep stitching even by having the edge of the foot level with the fold. It can of course be made narrower in fine fabrics; adjust the width by moving the needle position off centre. Leave long ends of thread at one end. To turn right side out, insert a rouleau needle, sew the eye to the corner of the rouleau using the ends of thread. Ease fabric on to needle and pull out.

VARIATION ON DRE
NO. 2: A sweetly tuck
and edged bridal dress us
the panel bodice, below-ell
sleeves and six-panel skirt w
deep hemline flounce. Mix li
of ribbon and flat tucks, ad
ing a central band of bea
or pearls. Alternative
work lines of machine e
broidery. Work the deco
ation before cutting
to size. On the sk
panel tuck the cen
only or arrange in
shape to fit the par
Add eyelet edging
panels, sleeve he
and frill sea
bead the belt
match the dr

Use synthetic thread such as Drima; it will not split when rouleau is turned. Use rouleau for shoulder straps, hanging loops and for long loops at the waist of the boned bodice dress to hang it up. Rouleau can also be slip-stitched inside a lined coat or jacket as a decorative finish on the edge of the lining. Finish the ends with a knot, with beads or by tucking in the ends. It can also be used threaded through the loop of a pearl or crystal button.

SCALLOPS, SHELL EDGING AND TUCKS

Scallops

Faced scallops are suitable only for crisp opaque fabrics. Use at the hemline of overdress layers;

could also be used on both edges of a wide stiffened cummerbund. Adopt the same technique for a head-dress, clutch bag etc.

Cut out with edges straight, join all seams except one. The seam left open should be at the side, not the centre back. Decide approximately what size scallop you want, measure the length of the garment edge and adjust the size until you are sure you will fit in a number of whole scallops. Find a plate, saucer, table mat etc. of that size and either use it as a template – sticking pieces of basting tape at the edge to mark the extent of the curve you will use – or make a cardboard template.

Press a strip of iron-on Vilene to the wrong side of the garment 3cm (1¼in) deeper than the scal-

Make the backs of all the dresses interesting for church weddings.

lop. Outline the scallops on the Vilene, using a fabric pen. Stitch the garment seam, adjusting the amount of seam allowance so that the scallops match. Cut a piece of fabric 1.5cm (⅝in) deeper than the Vilene and baste it right side down to right side of garment. Join the ends to match the garment seam, press open. Stitch along outline. Trim to within 5mm (¼in) of stitching, snip frequently and snip right to the corners between the scallops. Roll the facing to the wrong side, work the join to the edge and tack. Press. Trim and neaten the raw edge of the facing.

There are several ways of hold-

DRESS DESIGN NO. 2

The panelled bodice with full sleeve to below elbow with elastic casing. The bodice fastens with five buttons and loops at the back seam. The skirt has six panels cut to shorter length with deep frill attached.

Pattern (see drawings page 121)
PIECES: 2, 3, 4, 5, 6, 7 for bodice
8(B) for sleeve
1(C) for skirt plus frill – this combination is also suitable for a petti-coat.

Cutting out

Cut out six skirt panels to length. Cut nine pieces for the frill, each 90 cm (36in) wide and 40cm (15¾in) deep. Cut front and back bodice panels on double fabric;

cut neck facings to fold. Cut two sleeves. Mark centres of skirt panels, centre front of bodice. Mark casing placement lines on sleeves. Cut facings in Vilene.

Making up

1. BODICE Attach Vilene to neckline. Stitch centre back seam to dot. Stitch panel seams on back and front bodice. Press front seams towards centre. Stitch shoulders. Attach neck facing. See p. 33. Stitch right side seam of bodice.

2. SKIRT Stitch skirt seams, leaving opening for zip at the waist of one seam. Join frill sections. Turn up and stitch the hem. Gather frill and attach to skirt. See p. 35.

3. WAIST Gather skirt and attach to bodice. See p. 54.

4. ZIP Insert zip in left side seam of dress.

5. SLEEVES Stitch sleeve seams. Turn up narrow hem round sleeve. Attach elastic either in a casing on the inside of sleeve or direct to the fabric. See p. 32. Gather sleeve head and attach sleeves to bodice. See p. 53.

6. BUTTONS AND LOOPS Arrange the buttons on the left of the back opening and sew in place. Make five loops from thread or rouleau and attach to right edge of back opening. Rouleau loop ends can be stitched neatly under the edge, or if you prefer the ends can be covered by hemming a bias strip over them. Remove all tackings from dress. Press.

ing back the facing: top stitching, with matching stitching round edges of scallops (this can be decorative stitching); attach a line of ribbon or lace to the right side, stitching through to the facing; you can use the lining to cover the facing edge, stitching them together; or use Wundaweb tucked under the facing and pressed.

Shell edgings

An effective finish on edges of frills, veils etc. and edges of sleeves. Not suitable for thick fabrics.

HAND SHELL HEM   Trim fabric edge, leaving 5mm ($\frac{1}{4}$in) seam allowance. Fold a small double hem on to the wrong side, tack and press. Stitch the hem by sliding the needle through the hem fold for 5mm ($\frac{1}{4}$in) or so, then take the needle right over the hem twice, pulling the thread to wrinkle the fabric slightly (below). If the fabric is springy, slide the needle through the fold for only 3mm ($\frac{1}{16}$in), take one hemming stitch and slide it for a further 3mm ($\frac{1}{16}$in). Remove tacking stitches very carefully. Press very lightly.

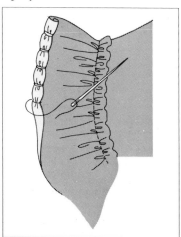

MACHINE SHELL HEM   Attach shell hem foot to machine, set to a suitable stitch. Trim fabric edge cleanly to leave slightly more than 5mm ($\frac{1}{4}$in) and feed it through the foot. Try this technique on spare fabric first, as there is a knack of holding the edge of the fabric upright as it goes over the foot.

An alternative method if you cannot master the shell hem foot is to tack the hem, then machine it with the same stitch, but make sure the needle goes well clear of the fold; this will pull the edge in and wrinkle it. On some fabrics like chiffon and voile, it will work better if you simply fold under the edge of the fabric once, without tacking, and stitch.

Tucks

Tucks can be made in groups or to cover an entire section such as bodice panel, cuff etc. Stitch all types of tucks before cutting out the pattern piece, so that the size and shape is accurate. Conventionally the raised side is the right side, but on a plain stiff fabric a slightly quilted effect is created by stitching the tucks on the wrong side. A square effect is produced by making a second series of tucks across the first at right angles. Use a piece of fabric that is at least 8cm (3in) longer than the pattern piece; you will have to estimate the width, but you should in any case make a sample to test the stitching; you can then make a calculation from that. Stitch on the lengthwise straight grain; use a small stitch and sew all tucks in the same direction. Do not reverse the stitching at the ends as this distorts the middle of the piece of fabric. If you use fabric with stripes, spots or lines in the weave, let the design govern the type, width and spacing of the tucks.

FLAT TUCKS   Can be used on any fabric, but probably most effective on those that are crisp and opaque. Fold fabric right side out exactly on the straight grain and press. If the weave of the fabric makes it difficult to see the grain when folded, make a line of dots using a fabric pen and ruler with fabric flat. Insert a few pins across the fold to prevent fabric slipping. Lower the machine foot with its edge on the fold and stitch to the end. Press the stitching flat. Open out the fabric and press the tuck to one side; press again on the wrong side. While still at the ironing board, fold the fabric for the next tuck, using an adjustable marker set to the distance you require from *stitching* of the previous tuck to the *fold* of the next. (This is a shorter distance than measuring from fold to fold, so it is easier to be accurate.) Fold the fabric with previous tuck on top and press the fold of the second tuck. Stitch the tuck; press it; mark the next one and so on.

Press either all in one direction or to each side of the centre front, adding buttons or embroidery in between. Rows of ribbon can be stitched between tucks; machine embroidery can be added to the edges, perhaps in a contrast coloured thread; ric-rac braid or lace can be stitched under the edges. Deep flat tucks can also be used horizontally round the skirt above the hem. On the small bridesmaid's pattern they can be stitched all round, as the skirt is straight. On the wedding dress skirt, keep the tucks fairly narrow as the panel is shaped, or make tucks in alternate skirt panels only.

PIN TUCKS   Use on any fabric but particularly effective on fine and transparent materials. Press the fabric in the same way as for flat tucks, but stitch with the needle right on the fold. Press the stitching, but leave the tuck standing upright. Mark the next and subsequent tucks with the first one still folded and measure from the fold, not the stitching.

TWIN NEEDLE TUCKS   Try out this technique, as it is less effective on thick or stiff fabrics than on soft materials. Select a size of needle with a needle space that is suitable for your fabric. Put the pin-tucking foot on the machine. Thread the machine with two reels of thread on top, one threaded through each needle. Coloured threads can be used. Straight zig-zag or decorative stitches can be adopted. Mark the straight grain on the fabric with a row of dots and stitch the first tuck. Move the fabric so that the tuck slots into a groove in the foot, spacing it as you wish. Stitch second tuck. Continue in this way. Press if necessary but do not flatten the tucks. A very attractive hem stitch can be produced by using a wing needle.

SEAMS

Plain open seam

Place fabric pieces with right sides together flat on the table if possible; match balance marks and tack 1.5cm ($\frac{5}{8}$in) from the edge. Begin at the hem and stitch towards waist or neckline. If fabric is slippery or if you cannot lay out the entire seam on the table, insert a few pins across the seam allowance. With fabrics that move even when tacked, such as chiffon and slipper satin, it helps to leave the pins in until you stitch the seam by machine. Alternatively with easy fabrics, long straight seams, frill joins etc., dispense with tacking and insert pins across the seam every 15cm (6 in) or so. Make sure the pin heads extend to the right of the raw edge so that you can quickly remove them as you reach them when stitching. Machine-basting is another alternative for long seams, pinning first if fabric is slippery. Stitch the seam from hem to waist or neck, reversing at the start and finish to anchor the thread. Avoid the possibility of seams splitting where others will later cross them by anchoring threads as follows: At the start of the seam stitch forward for 2cm ($\frac{3}{4}$in), reverse for almost 1cm ($\frac{3}{8}$in) and then continue stitching forward. At the far end stop and reverse again 1cm ($\frac{3}{8}$in) before you come to the end of the seam. This holds the stitching at the point where you need it; you will not be trimming off the reversing, so the seam cannot come undone. Remove

If the dress is made from one layer of plain fabric such as satin or crêpe, don't use narrow neck facings – these will be bulky and may show up denser than the remainder of the bodice. Instead, make two bodices and stitch them together round the neck, turning one through to the inside. The neck edge can then have lace or a decorative technique applied; a frill or piping could be inserted between the bodices, or the edge may be left pressed flat.

tacking. Press the stitching flat. Open out the fabric wrong side up and press open the seam allowances with your fingers. Press along the seam with the toe of the iron, then press again but lightly. With fabrics such as satin that are likely to show imprints, keep some strips of brown paper by the iron to slip under the seam edges before you press. Turn the fabric to the right side, press again if necessary, but protect shiny or delicate fabrics with a dry muslin cloth.

Neatening the edges

It is not necessary to neaten the edges of sections that will be lined. Unless the fabric frays badly you could neaten skirt seams for the lower 45cm (18in) only. Edges that must be neatened can be controlled with zig-zag or overlocking, or a softer flatter stitch that takes the thread over the edge less frequently is often more suitable. You need only turn under and edge-stitch the seam allowances if the dress is for a child and it is suitable for subsequent wearing and washing. Short seam edges can be overcast by hand or pinked. Whichever method you choose, work in the same direction as the seam stitching, i.e. hem upwards; you then go *with* the fraying and not against it. Do not reverse machine neatening at the ends. Re-press each end of the seam to flatten it ready to be joined to another section. It should not be necessary to press the entire seam again.

   Adding binding to seam edges adds bulk and may only be necessary on certain areas such as the waist, but if you want to do it use knit binding or net. Fold knit binding, wrap evenly over seam edges and stitch through all layers with zig-zag. Cut strips of soft dress net 1.5cm (⅝in) wide, make any joins by overlapping the ends and stitching across. Fold strips down the centre and press. Slip the strip over the raw edge and attach with one row of zig-zag or other stitch, set to a width of about 1 on the dial.

Narrow seam

Place pieces of fabric right sides together and insert pins diagonally through the layers at intervals of about 15cm (6in), but positioning them at least 5cm (2in) within the raw edges. Carefully trim 1cm (⅜in) from the raw edges. Insert more pins across the seam close to the edge, with heads extending to the right. This seam would normally be used on fine fabrics, so leaving in the first row of pins will help to keep the layers together. Set the machine to a full width overlock or other straight-with-zig-zag stitch and sew from hem to waist or neck, making sure the needle clears the raw edges when it moves to the right. If the edges curl up, reduce the stitch width.

Use a very narrow seam on transparent fabrics. Pin the layers together and work a row of straight stitching 3mm (⅛in) outside the seam line, i.e. 13mm (½in) from the raw edge. Trim the fabric very close to the stitching. Stitch over this line of stitching with a small zig-zag. Press narrow seams flat, then press to one side but keep the iron off the stitched edge. Use the iron to push the fabric over rather than placing it on the top. Press the right side if necessary, but putting the iron on the single layer of fabric only, up against the seam and not over it.

If two narrow seams are to meet, make the join more accurate by pressing the seams in opposite directions to even out the bulk.

French seam

Put the pieces of fabric *wrong* sides together, pin if necessary and tack. Stitch halfway between the edge and the seam line, i.e. more than 5mm (¼in) but less than 13mm (½in). Remove tacking, press stitching flat. Open out fabric and press both seam allowances to one side, pressing the toe of the iron against rather than over the top. Carefully trim the raw edges to less than 5mm (¼in). Roll one layer of fabric over until they are both right sides together; use your fingers to get the seam line on the edge, then tack 5mm (¼in) from the edge. Stitch beside the tacking, but first hold the seam up to the light to make sure that the fraying edge will be enclosed. If not, make the line of stitching a little further away from the edge. Press the seam flat, then lightly to one side. Press right side only if really necessary.

Lace seam

Lap one piece over the other, matching the design as closely as possible; pin or tack. Oversew by hand or with a small zig-zag stitch, following a line of design. The less straight the line the less it will show. Trim away the surplus lace close to the stitching on both sides of the seam. Press on a terry towel.

Net seam

Lap one piece over the other and work a straight stitch 3mm (⅛in) from the upper raw edge. Change to a narrow zig-zag stitch and

Plan the position of all the pattern pieces but cut out only those you will be sewing on immediately. This saves the others from becoming creased or frayed, and also allows for changes of mind on the part of the bride. Do not leave pins in the remaining fabric; roll up the fabric with the pattern pieces in position.

stitch over the top of the straight stitch. On the underneath, trim away the surplus net. This seam can also be used for seams in Vilene and for petticoat seams in thick or non-fraying fabrics.

Piped seams

Prepare sufficient piping as described on p. 47. Use either soft piping or piping with cord inserted – both are equally effective. Make a small sample seam so that you can insert the piping accurately. Pin the piping to the right side of one piece of fabric with the raw edges within the raw edge of the fabric. Stitch the piping in place. For filled piping, attach the zip foot to the machine and sew as close as possible to the cord. For soft piping, stitch 3mm (⅛in) from the folded edge. In both cases this stitching must fall on the seam line or a fraction closer to the raw edge. When you have carefully measured the distance required from the raw edge to the folded edge of the piping, mark a line of dots on the dress seam and attach the piping. It is not necessary to tack it in place unless the seam is shaped or awkward to handle, e.g. waist join. Press the stitching, using the toe of the iron. Place the second piece of fabric right side down on the piping with raw edges level.

Tack to prevent the edges slipping. *Turn the seam over* and work a row of stitching on top of the first row or a fraction further from the raw edge. Remove tackings, press the stitching if you can but without pressing on the piping. Trim the seam allowances. They can be neatened together at the waist, but elsewhere reduce bulk by pressing one seam allowance in the other direction. Where filled piping meets another seam, zip etc., remove the last 1cm (⅜in) or so of the cord to reduce bulk and make a neater end.

SLEEVES

Setting in sleeves should be the final process on the bodice for dresses with long skirts. Make up the sleeve completely. Insert a gathering thread over the top of each sleeve, using a large straight machine stitch and putting it slightly less than 1.5cm (⅝in) from the edge. With bodice and sleeve right side out, put underarm seams together and pin. Pin together from there as far as the ends of the gathering thread, keeping raw edges together and taking care not to stretch the sleeve edge. Tack the underarm with small stitches, fasten off the thread, remove pins (top). Put your hand inside the bodice and take hold of the centre of the sleeve head and the end of the shoulder seam. Pull the bodice over until it is wrong side out with the sleeve inside the hollow of the armhole. Flip over the two layers so that the sleeve edge is on top and insert a pin across the shoulder seam. Still with the sleeve on top, pull up the gathering thread and wind the end round a pin. Even out the gathers

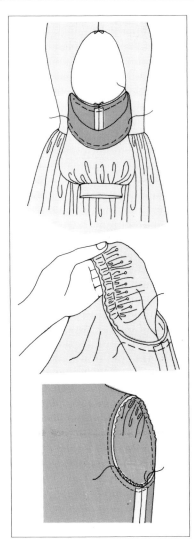

over the top of the sleeve. Insert pins at close intervals across the sleeve (centre). Tack over the sleeve head. Remove pins.

To stitch in the sleeves, slide the armhole under the machine foot, gathers uppermost. Begin near the underarm and stitch slowly round just beside the tacking. Stop every three or four stitches and re-position the seam; smooth out the fabric beneath and, over the sleeve head, even

out the gathers. Remember you are sewing round a circle. If you are nervous of putting in sleeves or the fabric is difficult to handle or bulky, it would be worth sewing round with a large hand backstitch first, removing all tackings etc., and then machine stitching round on top.

Trim seam allowances to tidy them, not to reduce them in width; neaten them together with zig-zag or bind with knitted binding (bottom). Push the seam allowance towards the sleeve head for support. Press on the right side with the toe of the iron on the bodice and only just touching the seam all round to smooth it. The gathering threads will help to hold the gathers up stiffly, but if they show on the right side they will have to be removed. If using lace, chiffon etc., trim seam to 3mm (⅛in) and neaten with a tiny zig-zag or a narrow self-finish seam.

Support for sleeve head

A soft support can be made as follows and attached to the sleeve after cutting out but before joining the seams. Unsuitable for transparent fabrics. Cut a piece of dress fabric on the bias, one and a half times the length of the edge of the sleeve that will be gathered, and 5cm (2in) wide. Fold it wrong side inside and press. Insert a gathering thread along the raw edges. Tack it to the wrong side of the sleeve head with raw edges level, pulling up the gathering thread and easing the fabric round the curve. Machine stitch in place, remove tackings. Make up the sleeve and insert it in the armhole in the usual way, gathering it up to fit.

Make a stiffened sleeve head

support as follows, inserting it in the sleeve after it has been attached to the bodice. Not suitable for transparent fabric. Use firm iron-on Vilene and dress fabric or lining. Cut two pieces of Vilene oval in shape, measuring about 10cm (3¾in) across the width and the length of the gathering over the sleeve already stitched in the bodice. Press each piece to the wrong side of the fabric and cut out. Fold each piece in half and zig-zag round the edge. Fold back 1cm (⅜in) along the straight edge and insert in the armhole under the seam allowance. Match the centre of the support to the shoulder seams, pin to the seam allowance. Sew in place, using hand back stitch or machine stitching. Hold it with armhole uppermost and support it underneath so that the armhole is kept in shape. Folding the edge in this way to extend the straight edge in addition to the curved edge will ensure that it remains rigid. The support can also be padded by placing a sausage shape of polyester wadding on the oval pieces of fabric before folding and stitching.

WAISTLINES

Complete the bodice finishing the seams and neckline. If it is a full-length dress, set in the sleeves. Mark the waistline on the bodice at fitting by putting a piece of tape or curved petersham round and mark position on bodice with a row of tacking stitches. If piping is to be inserted in the waist, stitch it to the right side of the bodice. Cut a piece of tape or knitted binding, or cut a length of selvedge from lining fabric exactly the same length as the waist edge

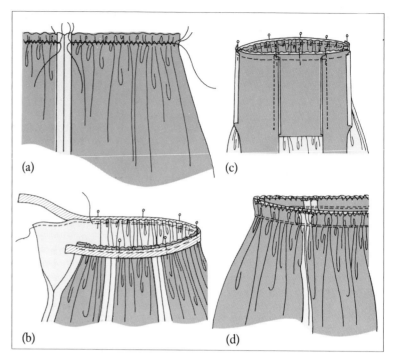

(a) (b) (c) (d)

of the bodice. Fold into eight and mark with fabric pen.

Stitch and finish skirt seams, insert gathering threads, one to each skirt panel (a). If there is more than one layer to the skirt, tack them together round the waist before inserting the gathering threads. Except on fine fabrics such as chiffon and voile, use fine crochet cotton or buttonhole twist, couching it in place with zig-zag. Mark skirt waist edge into eight; these marks may correspond with the seams if you have eight panels, if not mark with fabric pen. Pull up each gathering thread for some distance to ruche the fabric. Pin the tape to the wrong side, matching the eight marks. Work on one section at a time, pull up the gathering thread until the skirt fits the tape and wind the end of thread round a pin to hold it. Push the gathers along to even them out. Insert

plenty of pins across the tape. Pull up the gathering thread more if necessary. Tack the section from the right side to ensure that the stitches fall a fraction below the gathering thread. Feel for the tape underneath and pass the needle through it with each stitch (b). Fasten off the tacking. Remove pins. Move on to the next section; pin, gather and tack and so on along each section. Stitch the tape to the skirt, stitching with gathers uppermost. Remove all tackings and pull out the gathering threads. Re-mark waist edge into four parts; mark waist edge of bodice into four. Attach bodice to skirt, placing them right sides together, matching waistline to skirt stitching and matching the quarters. Pin and tack (c). You may need to tack twice if the fabric is heavy. After fitting, stitch round the waist twice for strength, sewing close to the first row in the skirt. Remove tackings (d). Trim edge and zig-zag or bind with knitted binding; or use edge of bodice lining, turning it under and hemming into the machine stitches.

ZIPS

The zip is inserted in the left side seam of the adult dress pattern so that it will not be seen. Use either the overlap or edge-to-edge method. If you decide to put the zip in the back of the dress an invisible zip is best as no stitching then appears on the outside. The method for inserting this type of zip is described below.

The bridesmaid's dress has a centre back zip. Insert by any of the methods shown below.

The sweetheart neck version of the adult dress has a short neckline zip in the back seam which should be inserted by the edge-to-edge method. This method can also be used if you decide to use a zip to fasten the opening at the wrist of the fitted sleeve.

Prepare the seam for all methods by marking guide points on the fabric edges. To do this place edges together and machine from one to the other for 1cm (⅜in) or so, stitching 2cm (⅔in) below the raw edges at the neck or armhole. Snip the thread between the two to detach them. Mark points on the zip tape to correspond. Use fabric pen and make a mark each side of the teeth 5mm (¼in) above the top stop of the zip.

Zips can be stitched in place by hand, using prick stitch for outside stitching or back stitch if it is inside; or with a medium length straight stitch and using a zip foot on the machine. If you prefer the appearance of hand sewing, sew along the edge of the tape by machine, working a small zig-zag stitch to attach it to the seam allowance, after hand stitching near the teeth. Do not use pins; use basting tape. Establish the fitting line accurately at the fitting and mark the lines with tacking or fabric pen.

If the dress is not to be lined, neaten the seam edges. Trim away the waist seam bulk for 2cm (¾in) on each edge.

Overlap method

Insert a narrow strip of fabric along each edge to prevent a wrinkled zip. Use knitted binding, bias binding or light iron-on Vilene and press or baste with one edge on the marked seam line.

On back bodice place zip face down on right side of fabric, matching marks on tape to balance mark on seam edge. The edge of the teeth should run on the seam line. Tack and stitch from top to bottom, using the zip foot on the machine. Remove tacks, roll zip until it is right side up, fold fabric edges back and tack close to teeth through all layers. Baste lining in place beside zip and round armhole. Trim raw edge, turn under, tack to zip tape.

On front of dress at underarm fold edge under, tack and press. Bring this edge over the zip, covering the teeth, match balance marks and waist seams and oversew in place. Tack tape beside teeth through dress and zip tape, or hold with basting tape. If you need a straight line on which to stitch, mark a line of dots with fabric pen. Stitch the zip, starting at the bottom. Do not sew across the bottom, it causes a bulge. Remove tackings. Press the stitch-

ing with toe of iron only after removing all tackings. If bodice is lined, bring lining into place on wrong side, baste beside zip and round armhole. Turn under the edge, tack and hem lining to zip tape.

If the dress has an overlay of lace or chiffon, insert side seam zip in two stages; first from underarm to waist through both layers; then lift the overlay out of the way and insert remainder of zip attaching to under layer only.

Invisible zip

Stitch garment seam, neaten edges. Stitch up remainder of seam, using a large machine stitch and making sure waist seams match. Press seam open. Place zip right side down on back of seam, matching balance marks to zip marks. Tack zip tape to seam allowance or hold down with basting tape. Remove the big stitches in the seam; they will pull out easily. Undo the zip. Stitch close to the teeth, using zip foot. Stop and fasten off at lowest point. Stitch the second side. Close the zip. Complete the stitching at the base by sewing the tape to the seam allowance. This can be done by hand. Do not press this zip. If the bodice is lined, bring lining into position, trimming the edges and turning under and hemming to the tape.

At the armhole edge oversew the seam edges together above the zip.

Use Stitch'n'Tear embroidery paper underneath machine embroidery. It adds weight and avoids puckering. You need not necessarily tear away the backing afterwards.

Avoid the emergency of a broken zip by eliminating the waist strain. Stitch a length of 5mm (¼in) taffeta ribbon all round the waist to the seam allowance, sewing along one edge. Fasten off the stitching 3cm (¼in) from the zip. Trim ribbon ends, leaving them 40cm (16in) long. When the dress is put on, tie the ribbon in a bow to draw the dress in to the waist, then fasten the zip safely over the top.

If the dress needs altering after the zip is in, adjust the centre back seam rather than unpick the zip.

Edge-to-edge method

Stitch the garment seam and fasten off the stitching. Stitch the remainder of the seam where the zip is to go but using a large machine stitch or small tacking stitches. Press open the seam. Neaten the raw edges for the entire length of the seam. If you are using French seams snip the seam at the top of the stitching, press the seam allowances flat above the seam, then stitch together and neaten as described above.

With seam wrong side up, place the zip right side down over the seam. Match up the guide points on the zip and seam, centralize the teeth over the seam and then tack along the middle of the tape to attach to the fabric. On fabrics that are not transparent, basting tape may be used instead of tacking stitches.

With fabric right side up stitch by hand or machine on each side of the zip teeth. Stitch in the same direction on each side; do not stitch across the bottom of the zip. Remove tacking stitches. Press the stitching with the toe of the iron.

Fitting

Although fitting is very important, it is largely a matter of common sense and not something to be nervous about. The following advice may help if you are not very experienced.

SIZE

Find out what size patterns or clothes the bride (or bridesmaid) usually has. Ask if she has any recurring problems resulting from her figure – for example, long arms, narrow shoulders and so on.

CHECKING

It is a great help to borrow from her something that fits, especially if she lives some distance away or if you have to make the dress without seeing her at all. Use the borrowed garment to check such items as back neck to waist, shoulder length, size of cuff, position of bust dart.

Making a toile will be the quickest way of experimenting. It is the only sure method of deciding on a style, especially if the bride wants to look taller, shorter, thinner, younger, more sophisticated etc. Use any white fabric such as muslin, with structured bodice parts in sew-in Vilene; or use a couple of old sheets.

TOILE

Although it is useful to make a toile first, especially if the style features have not been finally decided upon, this is time consuming and laborious. You may prefer to make a complete toile if the dress has to be despatched for fitting elsewhere, but otherwise combine fabric and toile as follows using inexpensive cotton muslin or old sheet, or else Vilene. Cut and fit the skirt in fabric unless features such as train, overskirt or panels are to be experimented with, in which case cut out those pieces only as a toile and the remainder in fabric.

Cut and fit the bodice as a toile if you have not made anything for the person before, or if you or she knows that she has a particular fitting problem.

Make a toile of the bodice if the fabric is particularly delicate or liable to be marked, or if you know it will be impossible to buy more – for example, if it is an heirloom or was purchased abroad.

If any part is to be made from contrasting fabric, make a toile for early fittings. For example, if the sleeves are to be made from chiffon or the bodice from sequinned fabric, cut that part only in toile fabric; make all adjustments, including marking armhole edges etc. The contrast fabric will then be fitted only once when the entire bodice has been put together. This advice applies to the decorated front bodice of the panel design dress in this book; carry out all early fittings with that panel tacked in place but use lining, Vilene etc.

PROPORTION

Adjust the pattern or the toile by lengthening or shortening if necessary in the following positions, remembering to leave hem and seam allowances untouched.

SKIRT: 25cm (10in) above hemline
BODICE FRONT: 8cm ($3\frac{1}{4}$in) above waist for short waist
15cm (6in) above underarm for hollow chest
BODICE BACK: 5cm (2in) above waist for hollow back (lengthen only)
8cm ($3\frac{1}{4}$in) above waist for short waist
8cm ($3\frac{1}{4}$in) below shoulder to lift for hollow back (instead of above waist)
SLEEVE: 8cm ($3\frac{1}{4}$in) above lower edge on full sleeve
8cm ($3\frac{1}{4}$in) below armhole on fitted sleeve.

Adjustments of up to 4cm ($1\frac{1}{2}$in) can be made in these positions, 13cm (5in) on the skirt. If the amount to be added or deducted is more than this, make two alterations 5cm (2in) apart in order to maintain the correct balance and shape of the pattern.

Remember to reduce the proportion of additional features to correspond. If the skirt has a deep hemline frill make half the adjustment on the main part and the remainder on the frill by reducing its depth; on the fitted sleeve, reduce the depth of the cuff slightly if the sleeve is shortened.

If several people are to wear the same design, remember to adjust each one. For example, the deep hemline frill must be less deep on someone very short, even if she is to appear beside someone tall who is wearing the same design. In order to overcome any obvious problems, it is an idea to modify the design – perhaps by omitting features that might overpower the smaller participants.

MEASUREMENTS

Take some basic measurements in order to select the pattern size and to make length adjustments, but it is easier to do all other fitting on the individual concerned. Remember that it helps to have the bodice inside out for the first fitting so that adjustments can be pinned accurately before being tacked and checked.

DRESS: DESIGN NO. 3

The panelled bodice with wide, shaped frill bound and set into back and front seams. The full sleeve to short length with elastic in casing. The overskirt is made of eight panels caught up at the seams; the underlayer has six panels but with deep frill. The back bodice has a deep square neck.

Pattern (see drawings page 121)

PIECES: 2, 3, 4, 5 for bodice
8(E) for sleeve
1(B) for overskirt
1(C) for underskirt plus frill
Shoulder frill from diagram pattern (p. 76).

Cutting out

Cut out six skirt panels for underskirt and eight for overskirt to appropriate hemlines. Cut frills for underskirt: nine pieces 90cm (36in) wide and 45cm (18in) deep. Cut out four bodice frill sections as shown. Cut front bodice to fold, cut back and front panels on double fabric. Draw a lower neckline on centre back panel. Cut the back to a seam, or fold back 1.5cm ($\frac{5}{8}$in) and cut to fold. Cut 2m50 ($2\frac{3}{4}$yd) bias fabric

2.5cm (1in) wide if not using bias binding.

Making up

1. BODICE   Stitch centre back seam. Bind neck edge of centre back and centre front bodice sections. See p. 25. Join each side front panel to side back panel at shoulders; stitch and press. Make hems at outer edges of frills. Gather frills, place right side down on right side of panel sections with raw edges level and attach with bias strip, hemming the bias on the wrong side to neaten.

Using an overlaid seam, place side panels on centre front and centre back sections, with right sides up and matching the waist edges. Tack and stitch close beside the edge of the binding, sewing through frill, side panel and centre panel. Stitch right side-seam of bodice.

2. OVERSKIRT   Join skirt panels, leaving opening for zip at waist edge of one seam. Turn up hem of overskirt. Insert a gathering thread along alternate seams to a depth of 30cm (12in), but do not draw up until dress is complete as it is difficult to press out any

creases. An alternative method of drawing up the skirt is to leave a gap in the seam above the hemline and thread ribbons through to be tied in bows.

3. UNDERSKIRT   Join skirt panels, leaving a gap for zip. Join frill sections; make hem on frill; gather frill and attach to underskirt. Put underskirt inside overskirt with waist edges level and tack. Machine together if heavy. At base of zip opening, snip seam allowances as far as stitching and press outwards, then fold back over the edge of the opening in the underskirt. Tack. Gather skirt and attach to bodice. See p. 54.

4. ZIP   Insert zip in side.

5. SLEEVES   Stitch sleeve seams. Turn up sleeve hems and stitch. Attach casing and insert elastic or stitch elastic to wrong side of sleeve. Gather sleeve head, attach sleeve to bodice. Remove all tackings from dress. Press.
Note: If the two skirts together are bulky, join overskirt only to bodice and make underskirt separately, turning 2.5cm (1in) hem at the waist as a casing and inserting elastic.

VARIATION ON DRESS NO. 3: A luxurious Regency look results from using ruffles, lace and bows. The centre of the panel bodice is tucked with a central band of lace, the shoulder frill is lace layered on fabric, repeated on the below-elbow sleeve between elastic line and hem with ribbon applied to bodice seams and to the tucked belt. An eight-panel skirt is looped over a six-panel frilled underskirt and the look is completed with a parasol and rouleau or ribbon bows scattered over dress and veil

Buy a new box of pins; special bridal pins are available, which are long and fine. Make sure you have some with coloured heads too – they are useful for fitting and can be found more easily in lace and velvet.

Take the opportunity to buy a couple of packets of fine machine needles; you will use up at least two needles on each dress. See fabric glossary for size.

Borrow a pair of pinking shears if you do not already have them and pink as many edges as you can in the skirt, lining and pet-ticoat. Neaten seam edges on skirt, lining and petticoat only above the hem, then use pinking shears up to the waist on the remainder. Avoid doing unnecessary amounts of detailed time-consuming sewing.

Pattern size

Take the measurement round the fullest part of the bust with the tape held firmly. Look at the size chart and select the pattern which is nearest to that measurement. If the latter falls between sizes, select the smaller one. When the person has a bust that is above average size and out of proportion, choose a smaller size that will fit her back, waist, shoulders, etc., but make additional seam allowances when you cut out the front bodice.

LENGTH: Measure from waist to hem (shoes on)
Measure from back of neck to waist.
Measure from underarm to waist at the side
Measure the sleeve seam of a garment that has a similar style sleeve, i.e. full or fitted.

Compare these measurements with those on the size chart and calculate the adjustments to be made.

OVERALL EFFECT

Put the adult dress on a dummy or dress stand to see the overall effect. Let the bride or bridesmaid see it too. It will not matter too much if the dummy is not the right size, but it should be adjusted to the appropriate height.

Fit bride's and bridesmaids' dresses early in the evening in order to give yourself time to adjust, re-tack and re-fit the same night; then you can carry on with the sewing. Otherwise you will be stuck next day, unable to get on if they are at work or school.

COMFORT

Remember the secret of all fitting is that a good fit is comfortable to the wearer; this rests more on getting the length right between the different parts of the body. Width is adjusted more for appearance than fit. Close-fitting and loose styles will feel comfortable if the proportion is right, but uncomfortable if the skirt is too long, the waist too high, the armhole too deep or the sleeves too long.

Fit one area at a time: bodice, bodice with sleeve, then bodice and skirt. Always try it on again after tacking an adjustment, but attempt to go a stage further somewhere on the dress so that you feel some progress has been made.

Panel bodice

designs 1, 2, 3, 4
BACK: Check panel seams run smoothly. Take in for narrow back; let out for broad back; take in below shoulder for protruding shoulder blades.
Check neckline level. Lift shoulder seams to raise; scoop out to lower.
Check length at waist. Lift shoulder seams to raise; lower them to lower the waist.

FRONT: Check panel seams run smoothly over fullest part of bust; adjust for a particularly high or low bust. Let out for large bust, take in for small. Take in at neckline for narrow chest. Take in at waist if necessary (this also gives more shape at bust).
Check neckline depth and width, remembering seam allowance is to come off. Raise shoulders to lift waist or to remove surplus across chest or above waist.

Make the toile in lining fabric and do the fitting adjustments on that to save handling the dress fabric too much.

SIDES: Check fit below armhole, adjust.

SHOULDERS: Re-slope if necessary. Release at armhole end for square shoulders; slope more for sloping shoulders. Keep shoulder seams running on top of shoulder.

ARMHOLE: Look at position of armhole edge; note any adjustment that might be needed when sleeve is tacked in.

Blouson bodice

designs 6, 7
BACK: Check back seam and neck; take in seam for narrow back or shoulders.
Check length and amount of blousing. Raise shoulders for short waist.

FRONT: Check length and level of bust dart; adjust. For prominent bust make dart wider at base.
Check V-neckline level, remembering seam allowance is to come off. Lift shoulders to raise (this will raise dart as well).
Check length to waist and also amount of blousing.

SIDES: Take in or let out side seams if necessary.

SHOULDERS: Re-slope if necessary. Make more sloping for sloping shoulders, less so for square shoulders, keeping seam along top of shoulder.

ARMHOLE: Look at position of armhole edge; note any adjustment that may be necessary when tacking in sleeves.

If a substantial alteration is made to the armholes, by adjustments to the sides or shoulders, the armholes should be re-cut. To do this re-pin the pattern pieces, with side edge level with dress seam, and recut. If the person is very small around bust and armhole, take a small pleat across the pattern halfway down the armhole on back and front, before re-pinning.

Fitted bodice

designs 5, 7, 8, 9.

BACK: Check level of upper edge; make a note to take small seam allowance if it needs raising.

FRONT: Check seams run over bust; adjust if necessary, taking in seams above bust for tighter upper edge (will also give more bust shaping). Take in below bust for smaller waist (will also give more bust shaping).

SIDES: Take in or let out to fit.

SHOULDER STRAPS: Adjust length. Adjust position if necessary although they look neatest when meeting in panel seam.

Waist level

At the second fitting, tie a piece of tape or ribbon round the waist over the bodice to mark the waist level. Mark the bodice level with the lower edge. Remember to blouse the bodice with darts over the tape as far as necessary.

Sleeves

CHECK LENGTH: If too long, pin out a pleat below the armhole, across the sleeve. Re-cut top of sleeve, using pattern but placing it lower. Allow for hem finish. If sleeve is too full, pin out underarm seam.

CHECK CUFF OR LOWER EDGE: Overlap each cuff to fit in case wrists vary; mark extension allowed. Remember to allow for bracelets.

CHECK ARMHOLE: Armhole must not be too deep; if it is, raise shoulders and reset sleeve. Seam must run in a straight line over the shoulder bone at the front. Take in or let out in small amounts over the shoulder and at back and front to remove any bodice overhang or tightness. Reset sleeves.

Skirt

CHECK: That all seams hang straight from waist. Adjust gathers if necessary to suit the figure. If the skirt drops at back or front adjust waist level of bodice.

If the skirt is too full, take out one panel and re-adjust and redistribute the gathers. Make sure the petticoats fit and that the wearer can walk, sit, kneel and so on.

Accessories

At the third fitting try on accessories, train, belts etc. to get the full effect. If these are not yet made substitute a piece of fabric or Vilene. At final fitting include veil and all decorations and accessories.

Making fitting adjustments

Where a seam is pinned, insert more pins on the under side picking up only one layer of fabric. Release first row of pins, keeping top layer of fabric on the point. Re-insert through that top layer. Tack over the pins, straightening the line if it is a straight seam or edge. Alternatively mark with fabric pen. Put seams together and re-tack.

Bridesmaids and other attendants

Brides often want even quite small bridesmaids to be dressed like the bigger bridesmaids or similar to the bride herself. Two basic patterns are therefore included, both of which can be varied in a number of ways, both designs are high-waisted to suit all ages and sizes, and both echo the line of the bigger pattern.

The panel bodice has a centre panel back and front with a cut-off line for a square neck to echo the bride's dress if you wish. This would be the best choice of style for chubby girls. Shaped shoulder frills can be inserted in the panel seams or the panel can be decorated. If the round neck is used the neck frill can be attached. There are neck facings for both round and square neck.

Make sure the bride and brides-maids know how to hold their flowers; baskets are especially tricky.

The plain bodice also has two necklines, the high one can have a single or double collar attached, the lower one can have the frill added. With both bodices trim the pattern on the chosen neckline, or if the pattern is needed again, trace off the piece of pattern before cutting the neckline. Both bodices are fastened with a zip in the centre back seam extending into the skirt seam.

The sleeve is long and full with elastic at the wrist. There is a cut-off line for a short sleeve and also, if you wish, the long sleeve can be made with a cap to echo the adult sleeve of the same style.

There is one pattern piece for the skirt which is cut to a fold for the front and to a seam at the centre back. The skirt can be plain and full length, plain short length, full length with a deep frill or full length with waist peplum to echo the adult style.

All pattern pieces are multi-size from 5–10. The pieces from each size can be combined in any way

Don't give little bridesmaids separate petticoats. It is safer and more comfortable to attach the petticoat to the waist of the dress, or simply to add a deep frill to the inside of the skirt of the dress.

you wish; there are many other simple variations that you will be able to make up yourself. Use the skirt pattern for petticoats, turning in and stitching a casing at the waist for elastic.

Any of the decorative techniques described in the book can be applied to the bridesmaid's designs and you can add flowers, bows, rosettes, ribbons and sashes as desired. Use the same pattern pieces if making overskirts, sleeves etc. in contrast fabrics.

If all the bridesmaids are bigger than the bride, keep them in pale colours.

BRIDESMAID'S DRESS NO. 1

Plain bodice with collar, long sleeve, short skirt.

Fabric and haberdashery

(see chart page 118)

Pattern (see drawings page 122)

PIECES: 27, 28, 24, 25 for
bodice
26 for sleeve
21(C) for skirt

CUTTING OUT   Cut skirt front to fold, cut pattern again to seam for the back. Cut 2 sleeves. Cut bodice front to fold, back to seam. Cut each collar pattern piece four times in matching or contrast fabrics for double collar.

VARIATION ON BRIDESMAID'S DRESS NO. 1: A demure version of the small bridesmaid's pattern with Peter Pan collar, long sleeves and tucked skirt. The butterfly shown on collar and skirt can be embroidered, beaded or appliqued or shadow stitched. Instructions are not given for the mob cap – it's simply two huge circles of fabric with soft Vilene between and gathered to loosely fit the head

For single collar cut upper collar only four times. Mark centre front on bodice and skirt. Cut 2 under collars in light Vilene unless fabric is transparent.

Making up

1. BODICE   Stitch shoulders and side seams. Press.

2. NECKLINE   Attach Vilene, if used, to wrong side of 2 collar pieces. Make up collars, attach to bodice neckline using bias strip.

3. SKIRT   Stitch back seam to zip point. Stitch side seams; press. Turn up and tack hem. Leave tacked until fitted

4. WAIST   Insert gathering thread round waist edge of skirt. Join bodice to skirt.

5. ZIP   Insert zip in centre back seam placing the slider at the base of the bias finish and trimming and neatening the ends of the zip tape. Attach small hook and thread loop above zip.

6. SLEEVES   Stitch sleeve seams. Press. Turn up and finish sleeve hems. Attach elastic to wrong side of sleeve, or attach bias casing and thread elastic through casing. Insert gathering thread over sleeve head. Attach sleeves to bodice.

Complete the hem. Remove all tacking stitches and press the dress.

Keep petticoats simple for bridesmaids as well as the bride. The petticoat should measure the same as the dress round the hem; have two narrower tiers above that. Make a waist casing for elastic; it is easy to tighten as everyone loses weight.

BRIDESMAID'S DRESS NO. 2

Plain bodice, frilled neckline, short sleeve, long skirt with hemline frill.

Fabric and haberdashery

(see chart page 118)

Pattern (see drawings page 123)

PIECES: 22, 23 for bodice
26 for sleeve
21(B) for skirt.

CUTTING OUT: Cut out skirt to fold for front; cut again to a seam for the back skirt. Cut front bodice to fold and back bodice to a seam. Cut 2 sleeves. Mark centre front of bodice and skirt.

Cut neck frill on the straight grain 90cm (36in) long and 8cm (3⅛in) deep. Cut bias strip 2.5cm (1in) wide for neckline.

Cut pieces for skirt frill 90cm (36in) long and 23cm (9in) deep. Cut 4 pieces for sizes 5, 6 and 7 and 5 pieces for larger sizes.

VARIATION ON BRIDESMAID'S DRESS NO. 2: For a young bridesmaid a long dress with dolly bag and rosettes for her hair as well as the dress. Basic bodice has lower neckline with frill; the sleeves are short; the skirt long with frill. Rosettes or ribbon roses secure the looped rouleau or lengths of contrast ribbon round waist and hem

Making up

1. BODICE   Stitch shoulders and side seams. Press.

2. NECKLINE   Make frill, gather and attach to neckline using bias strip. Make sure frill ends are 1.5cm (⅝in) within the centre back edges of the bodice to allow for inserting the zip.

3. SKIRT   Stitch back seam to zip point. Stitch side seams. Press. Join pieces for skirt frill. Turn up hem on frill and stitch. Gather upper edge and attach to skirt hem, first checking length.

4. WAIST   Insert gathering thread round waist of skirt. Join bodice to skirt.

5. ZIP   Insert zip in centre back seam placing slider below bias edge to minimise bulk. Trim ends of tape and neaten. Stitch zip holding ends of frill clear of stitching. Sew small hook and thread loop to fasten bias edging above zip.

6. SLEEVES   Stitch sleeve seams. Press. Turn up and finish sleeve hems. Stitch elastic to wrong side of sleeve or attach casing and insert elastic. Insert gathering thread over sleeve head. Attach sleeves to bodice. Remove all tacking stitches. Press dress.

BRIDESMAID'S DRESS NO. 3

Panelled bodice with square neck (shoulder frills optional), short sleeves, skirt with peplum.

Pattern (see drawings page 123)

PIECES: 31, 32, 33, 34, 37, 38
for bodice
26 for sleeve
21(A) for skirt plus
skirt to D cutting line
for peplum.

CUTTING OUT   Cut skirt pattern to fold for front and cut again to a seam for back skirt. Cut peplum once to fold for front and again to seam for the back. Cut centre front bodice to fold, cut front side panels, centre back panel and back side panels on double fabric. Cut two sleeves. Cut facings. Mark centre front of bodice, skirt and peplum.

VARIATION ON BRIDESMAID'S DRESS NO. 3: A short sleeve peplum dress for a young bridesmaid using the panel bodice. The centre panel can be smocked or shirred; the bodice seams, sash and hems of sleeves skirt and peplum bound with contrast or edged with ribbon

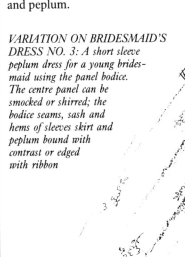

Making up

1. BODICE   Stitch (back and front panel) seams, inserting frills etc. if desired. Stitch shoulders. Press. Attach neck facings. Stitch side seams. Press.

2. SKIRT   Join centre back seam, join side seams. Join peplum side seams. Press. Turn up hem on main skirt and tack. Leave tacked until fitted. Turn up and stitch hem on peplum including centre back edges. Place peplum right side out over skirt, also right side out. Match side seams, centre fronts and waist edges. Tack together round waist, making sure finished edges of peplum at centre back are 1.5cm (⅝in) within the edges of the skirt to allow the zip to be inserted. Insert gathering threads along waist edge of skirt through skirt and peplum. Attach skirt to bodice.

3. ZIP   Insert zip in back seam. At neck edge lift facings clear of bodice and position the slider just below the neck seam. After inserting zip bring facings back into position on wrong side and stitch edges to zip tape. A hook should not be necessary above the zip unless you were unable to place the slider close to the neck edge. Tack and stitch zip from neck to waist then lift peplum clear of skirt seam. After stitching bring peplum down over zip.

4. SLEEVES   Stitch sleeve seams. Press. Turn up and stitch sleeve hems. Attach elastic to sleeve above hem or attach casing to sleeve and insert elastic. Insert gathering thread over sleeve head. Attach sleeves to bodice. Complete hem. Remove all tackings and press the dress.

Make sure bride and brides-maids buy their wedding-day bras in time for the first fitting. This is essential not only to ensure that the bodice fit is correct, but also to check that the straps don't show, and that the armholes are not too low if the style is sleeveless or sleeves are transparent.

PAGE BOYS

There can be few boys who enjoy being dressed in foppish clothes for a wedding; for most, the strain of taking part is enough. A compromise may have to be reached in order to reconcile the wishes of the bride with the feelings of a page boy, but he is likely to be more co-operative and less embarrassed if he is dressed soberly. In addition, it is sensible to provide him with an outfit that he can wear after the wedding in order to obtain maximum benefit from the outlay. Little girls, on the other hand, will want to wear their dresses constantly for dressing-up games and for going to parties. Ideas for compromise include:

Bow tie

Make the bow by folding a length of velvet ribbon and stitching it at the centre. Add a short piece of ribbon to the middle, wrapping it round the bow. Stitch the bow to a narrow band of petersham ribbon that will fit under the collar of a shirt. Fasten the band at the back of the neck with a small piece of Velcro or a press stud. Alternatively, make the bow from wide satin ribbon.

Shirts and trousers

Plain classic shirt, but in one of the colours of the wedding group, worn with trousers in coloured needlecord or cotton velvet – ruby or tomato red or dark green – or a lighter weight fabric such as poplin. Smart dungarees in needlecord; plain trousers but with a 'grandad' shirt.

Suits

Classic style jacket and trousers in black velveteen; waistcoat with breeches; trousers with a zip-front jacket that is not worn for the ceremony; all-in-one ice skater's suit; sailor suit that could be bought or made. But an easy alternative is to dress a boy in white shorts and socks and a white shirt to which you could add lines of narrow navy faille or grosgrain ribbon, even making a sailor collar that can be detached after the wedding.

Trousseau

KIMONO

Make a traditional kimono for the honeymoon. It can be full-length or thigh-length and belted with a sash or cummerbund. Select one of the decorative techniques in the book and apply to the bands, or choose one of the motifs and apply it to the kimono back. Use satin, crêpe, jaconne, with bands and lining in contrast colour. Sleeves could be lined with a third colour, even adding another pair of sleeves inside the first. Combine vibrant red, yellow, green or orange with black, or mix gentle rainbow colours; use textured fabric throughout, rather than lining material.

Pattern (see drawings page 123)

The kimono is in three sizes: *Small* which corresponds to dress sizes 8–10; *Medium* which corresponds to sizes 12–14, and *Large* which corresponds to sizes 16–18. Select the size required and outline the pattern as shown, either making a paper pattern first or outlining the shapes directly onto the fabric using tailor's chalk and a ruler. A seam allowance of 1.5cm ($\frac{5}{8}$in) is included all round.

Cut three rectangles of paper to sizes shown below. If you are cutting directly in fabric it should be folded double. Draw the back pattern with the centre back line on the fold of the fabric and arrange the pieces as shown in the illustration.

Note: The following details are for an ankle-length kimono, with measurements for a shorter-length kimono given in brackets.

FRONT AND BACK PATTERN

SMALL 147.5cm
(58in) × 28.5cm (11¼in)
(Short version 85.5cm
(33½in))

MEDIUM 149cm (58¾in) ×
30.5cm (12in)
(Shorter 87cm (34¼in))

LARGE 150.5cm (59¼in) ×
32.5cm (12¾in)
(Shorter 88.5cm
(34¾in))

BAND PATTERN

SMALL 157cm (62in) ×
19.5cm (7¾in)
(Short 95.5cm (37½in))

MEDIUM 158cm (62½in)
× 19.5cm (7¾in)
(Short 97cm (38¼in))

LARGE 160cm (63in) ×
19.5cm (7¾in)
(Short 98.5cm (38¾in))

SLEEVES: Cut rectangle 105cm
(41½in) × 30.5cm (12in)

SLEEVE BANDS: Cut rectangle
105cm (41½in) × 13cm (5in)

Complete the outlines as shown in
the illustration.

FRONT: From point A measure
8.5cm (3⅜in) along the shoulder.
Measure 24cm (9½in) down the
centre front line. Rule a line joining these two points; this is the
neckline. Measure 28cm (11in)
down the centre front from A and
draw a gentle curve between that
point and the neckline above as
shown. Mark underarm point
24.5cm (9¾in) down from
shoulder.

BAND: From point B measure
12cm (4¾in) along horizontal line.
Measure 33cm (13in) down from
B and join these two points. Mark

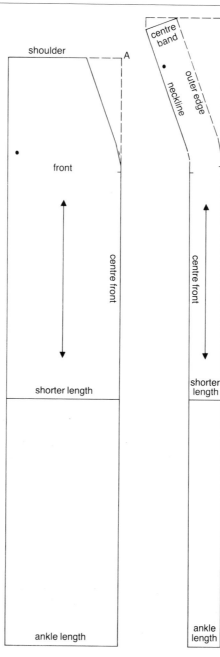

a point 4cm (1½in) below and
curve as shown. Mark the line
'outer edge'. Rule a line parallel
with the vertical edge and the
outer edge 8cm (3¼in) from it,
curving it at the base of the neckline to correspond with the front
line as shown.

pattern. Rule a line across the end
of the band and label it 'centre
back'. Mark the inner edge 'neckline'. Measure 10cm (4in) down
the neckline from centre back and
mark the point within the band.
This is the shoulder point.

BACK: Measure 1.5cm ($\frac{5}{8}$in) down centre back from C. Measure 7cm (2$\frac{3}{4}$in) along shoulder and join that point to the centre back point with a curve as shown.

Mark straight grain on each piece as shown.

Cutting out

In main fabric, cut out front on double fabric and back to the fold. Cut out sleeves on double fabric. Mark centre back with tacking. In contrast fabric cut four front bands and four sleeve bands; cut two sleeves, two fronts, cut the back to the fold.

Making up

Work desired decoration.

1. SLEEVES   With right sides together and edges level, stitch contrast bands to sleeves along one long edge. Press seams open (top). Stitch lining bands to lining sleeves and press. Fold each sleeve right sides together, matching underarm seam. Stitch seam, press open. Place linings and sleeves, right sides together, in pairs with band edges level and stitch round sleeve hemline. At opposite edge stitch round sleeve between dots; fasten off stitching (centre). Snip seam allowance as far as end of stitching. Trim raw edges where stitched, turn sleeve right side out. Tack stitched edges and press. Baste round armhole edges. Press lightly to crease the shoulder as a guide for attaching sleeves to kimono (bottom). If you wish to make a second pair of sleeves, do this now, slip them inside the main sleeves and baste all raw edges together.

2. BANDS   Place each pair of bands right sides together and stitch across centre back seam.

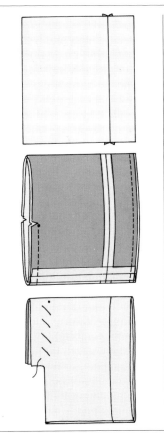

Press seam open. Join kimono shoulder seams, placing fronts on back with right sides together. Press seams open. Repeat on lining. Arrange the kimono on the table right side up and place contrast band on top right side down matching front edges and neckline. Match centre back seam to centre back of kimono, match shoulder point to shoulder seam and match at hemline. Tack and stitch outer edge. Trim, press seam allowances open on straight edges, towards band on curves. Join lining band to kimono lining in the same way.

3. SIDE SEAMS   Fold kimono right sides together, matching side seams, and stitch from hem to underarm point; fasten off stitching. Snip seam allowance

to end of stitching. Press seams open. Stitch lining seams similarly.

4. JOIN LINING TO KIMONO   With right sides together put lining to kimono and match all outer edges. Match centre back seams of bands, front edges, side seams and hem edges. Stitch round hem along front edges and round neck. Trim all edges, snip neckline and turn kimono lining right side out. Roll and tack all edges and press. Baste bands together and stitch by machine or by hand (prick stitch) in the seam line to hold bands together. At armhole edges baste kimono and lining together.

5. SLEEVES   With right sides together join armhole edge of kimono to sleeve edges; *exclude* kimono lining; *include* both raw edges of sleeve (below). Trim seam allowances and press towards kimono. Turn under raw edge of kimono lining and hem to cover armhole seam (bottom). Remove all tackings. Press.

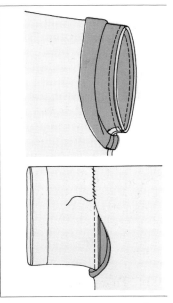

6. SASH OR CUMMERBUND   See p. 80.

ALL-IN-ONE

Pull-on drawstring suit with bands and back tie-fastening. Make it in a fabric that can be used with both sides as the right side or use a material such as satin and reverse it for contrast. Decorate the bands with any of the techniques described for the dresses, or substitute lace bands, or apply lace to fabric bands; use lace and ribbon for straps.

Pattern (see drawings page 123)

The suit is shown in three sizes, see Kimono for corresponding pattern size. Select required size and transfer pattern to squared paper, following the shape shown. You may find it easier to first trace off the outlines for your size, marking the measurements on the pieces before scaling up to full size.

Each square represents 2.5cm (1in). 1.5cm ($\frac{5}{8}$in) seams are allowed on all seams, 1cm ($\frac{3}{8}$in) on leg hems.

Cutting out

Cut out front bodice to fold, back bodice to seams. Mark centre front, mark depth of back opening. Cut out front and back leg pattern on double fabric. In main or contrast fabric, cut out bodice front band to fold, back band, front leg band, back leg band on double fabric. Cut two straps on the straight grain 60cm (23$\frac{1}{2}$in) long and 8cm (3$\frac{1}{4}$in) wide. Alternatively use ribbon for straps. Mark strap positions on bodice.

Making up

1. LEG SEAMS Join the two front sections at centre front and join the back sections. Place back against front and stitch side

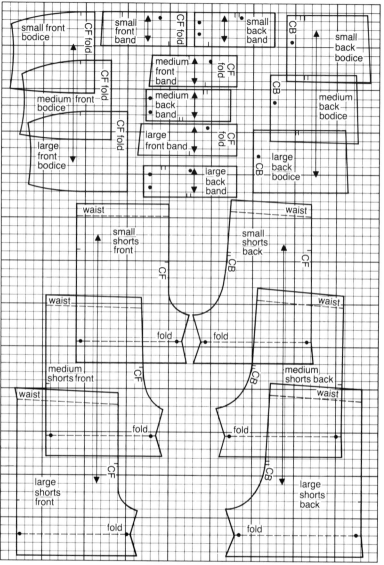

seams, stitching from waist as far as dot above hemline. Snip seam allowance as far as end of stitching. Turn leg right side out with remainder of seam allowance extending and stitch from end of stitching to hem. Trim and press.

2. CRUTCH SEAM Place back and front together, matching centre front and centre back seams. Stitch seam through crutch as far

as dot above hemline. Complete seam as for side seams.

3. HEMS Turn up hems, folding fabric on to right side and pressing. Turn in raw edge and tack to garment. Press. Stitch edge to complete. Decorative stitching, lace etc. can be added.

4. BODICE Stitch side seams. Stitch centre back seam to dot.

5. WAIST   With right sides
together join bodice to leg section,
matching side seams and centre
back and centre front. Take the
usual seam allowance on the
bodice but 3cm (1¼in) on the
shorts. Pin, tack and stitch. Press
waist seam allowances up towards
bodice. Tack from right side
round waist 1cm (⅝in) above waist
seam. Make a row of machine
stitching to the outside of the
tacking to form a casing. Leave a
2cm (¾in) gap near one sideseam.
Insert elastic in casing, pull up to
fit, join ends of elastic.

6. STRAPS AND BAND   Fold straps
right side inside and stitch long
edge. Turn right side out; press.
Place straps on wrong side of
bodice at strap positions with raw
edges level. Tack in position or
stitch (top). With right sides
together, join side seams of bands;
press. Place two ribbon or rouleau
ties 25cm (10in) long on wrong
side of bodice each side. Have tie
ends level with centre back edge
and place them 2cm (¾in) apart
with the upper tie 2cm (¾in) below
upper edge of suit (centre).

   Attach band to suit by placing
it on wrong side on top of straps
and ties with right side down.
Match upper edges, centre back
edges and seams and stitch round
the top and down the centre back
as far as the dot on the band
(bottom). Trim and snip edges.
Turn band to right side. Tack
and press round edge of suit.
Baste band in position. Turn in
outer edge; press, tack to suit.
Stitch along edge by hand or
machine. Remove all tackings.

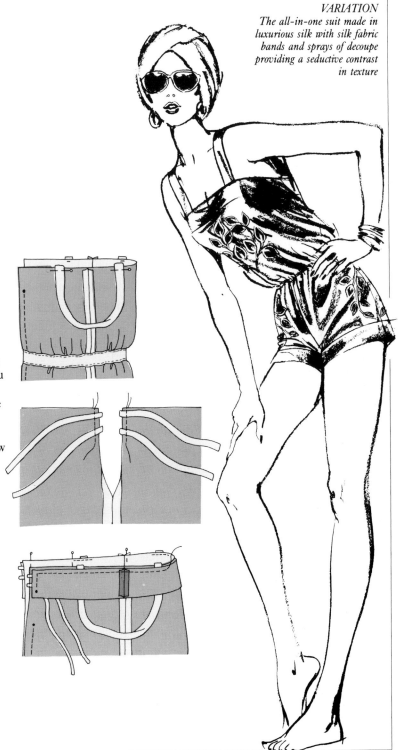

Accessories

PETTICOAT

A lighter weight cheaper fabric can be used, although polyester/cotton sheeting makes a good basic petticoat and is also wide. Another alternative is net, or net frills attached to a solid waist-to-hip section. Make the petticoat as simply and quickly as you can. *Complete it before the dress, so that you have it ready for fittings.*

Select from the following:

1. Basic petticoat

The basic skirt panel in the book can be used for a petticoat. Use three or more sections.

Join the seams, turn a casing at the waist and insert elastic. Turn up the hem. It can also be made with a frill at the edge, in which case shorten the pattern accordingly before cutting out.

2. Net petticoat

Cut a 3m (3¼yd) length of dress net into seven equal strips across the width. Join the ends of one strip to form the upper tier. Turn over the edge once for a casing; machine. Thread elastic through casing. Join together two more sections, gather along one edge and attach to upper tier. Make the four remaining strips into the bottom tier, gather and attach to the middle tier. At the hem, leave a cut edge or bind with satin bias binding or knit seam binding. When gathering net, use invisible thread: other threads shred when pulled. Use lapped seams, one raw edge over the other. A combination of fabric upper section plus net frill can be made.

3. Hooped petticoat

The width is important, so you may not be able to complete it before starting the dress. Make two sections. Measure the length you need the finished petticoat to be. Decide where you want the hoop; this may be slightly above the hem, or level with the upper edge of a hemline frill on the dress. Measure the width of the dress lining at that level and cut a rectangle of petticoat fabric slightly less in width, the depth you want plus 5cm (2in). Make a single or double frill deep enough to bring the join to hoop level and attach to one long edge of the rectangle. Fold right side inside and stitch from hem of frill to waist edge; sew lace etc. to lower edge. Measure correct length, turn over waist edge to form a casing. Insert elastic to fit waist. Try on petticoat and check that it is the right length. See Skirt lengths, p. 40. Attach bias binding or knit binding on the wrong side where the frill is joined on, stitching along each edge. Leave one end extending by 7cm (3in). Press the petticoat. Insert Rigilene poly-ester boning, then cut it leaving a short extension. Try on the petticoat under the dress to make sure the width is correct. Trim the Rigilene, trim the end of the binding, turn under and hem across it to prevent the boning from coming out.

VEIL

The simplest shape of veil is a circle folded not quite across the middle so that it forms two layers of differing lengths. Alternatives include an oval, even a folded square.

For a circular veil hanging to just below the waist at the back, cut a circle of veiling net 1m 60cm (62in) in diameter. For longer veils increase the measurement. A very fluffy veil could be made by using two circles or ovals of net of different sizes.

The main area of the veil can be plain or it can be embellished with pearls, sequins, embroidery etc., or, for a quick but effective decoration attach lace motifs using Bondaweb to stick them in place.

Buy accessories early to avoid disappointment at not finding what you had in mind. You will need the shoes in any case for dress fittings.

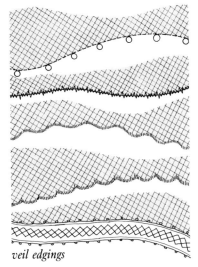

veil edgings

The edge of the veil can be clean cut or it can be bound or stitched. To attach binding fold and press the binding then fold it again right side out and press, shaping it to a curve to match the veil. Slot the edge of the veil between the edges of binding and machine using a zig-zag or decorative stitch that will penetrate the net and both edges of binding.

Hand sewn edgings include chain stitch embroidery and pearls. Machined edgings include scallops and other decorative stitches. Place the net on tissue paper before stitching.

TRAIN

A train can be either part of the back of the bridal dress, or it can be a separate floating section, made perhaps from chiffon or lace and attached at the back waist. A simple adjustment to the skirt pattern gives you the shape for both types. Another alternative is to attach a floating panel of lace or chiffon to the shoulders.

The integral train is faced round the hem edge, so you could also face the remainder of the dress hem or else it could be bound to correspond. A frill of fabric, lace etc. can be inserted round the edge of the train, the vertical shaped flounce can be added to the centre back or it can be embellished with any decorative process.

The floating train is made from two skirt panels and likewise can be decorated or have frills or edgings, or it can be made double – perhaps using a contrast colour on the underside. If you require a longer train, simply extend the pattern edges further.

Patterns

If you are satisfied with the appearance of the train as illustrated, you could pin the skirt pattern to the wrong side of the fabric, make the adaptation as shown in the diagrams (using tailor's chalk or fabric pen) and cut out. However, if you wish to experiment with the length, or are unsure about adapting the pattern, make the entire train pattern; this can be done either by using sheets of paper taped together or by making a toile from soft cotton muslin before cutting out in fabric.

Integral train: composed of four panels

1. Outline the skirt panel twice, adjusted to correct length. Fold in half, bringing side edges together, and crease. Open out the paper and mark the crease 'centre line'.

2. Working on one panel, mark a point 7.5cm (3in) inside the seam on both edges at the hem. Rule new seam lines from these points to the waist. Label the lines 'centre back' and 'side back' as shown.

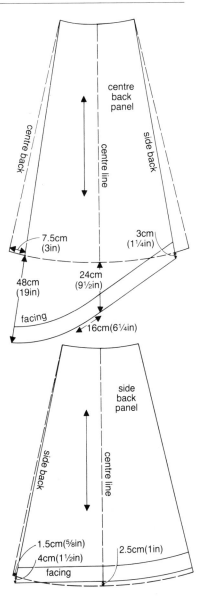

3. Extend the pattern as follows: Add 47.5cm (18¾in) to centre back. Add 24cm (9½in) to centre line. Add 3cm (1¼in) to side back.

4. Draw the train hemline by ruling a straight line from the bottom of the side back line, through the centre line and 16cm (6¼in) beyond. From there to centre back, draw a gentle curve as shown. If you intend to face the hem, draw a line 7.5cm (3in) above the new hem edge and trace off that piece separately.

5. Working on the second copy of the skirt panel, measure 1.5cm ($\frac{5}{8}$in) inside one edge at the hem, mark the point and rule a line to the waist. Mark this line 'side back', then extend it by 4cm (1$\frac{1}{2}$in).

6. At the centre line measure 2.5cm (1in) *up* from skirt hem and mark the point. Rule a straight line from this point to the side back line. Complete the train hem edge by drawing a curved line parallel with the original hem but 2.5cm (1in) above it.

machined edge finishes

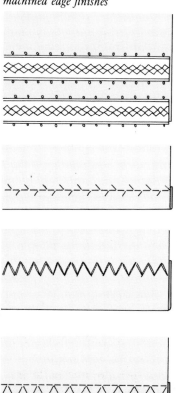

If you wish to face the hem, draw a line 7.5cm (3in) above the new hem edge and trace off.

Label this skirt pattern 'side back panel: cut 2'.
Label the first skirt pattern 'centre back panel: cut 2'.
Label each facing 'cut 2'.

Complete the skirt by cutting out four more panels for the front. If you wish to face the entire hemline, shorten the front panels by 2.5cm (1in) then make a facing by tracing a section off the skirt panel 7.5cm (3in) deep and cut out four times in fabric to face the front.

Remember that alternative materials can be used to face the hem such as Vilene, polypropylene braid, lining, cotton fabric, taffeta etc.

Floating train: composed of two skirt panels

1. Outline the skirt panel once. Follow instructions 1–4 above.

2. Label the pattern 'cut 2'. The skirt will be made up using the usual number of panels and the train will be added at the waist.

Floating train attached at shoulders

A simple and effective train can be made using a straight piece of fabric 115cm (45in) wide and 2m50 (2$\frac{3}{4}$yds) long – or longer if you wish. Scalloped lace or embroidered border fabric can be utilized provided the design is symmetrical.

Turn up a hem across one end 6cm (2$\frac{3}{8}$in) deep or on lace fabric zig-zag across it in a design to echo the lace and trim off the surplus. Alternatively a lace train can be made double, using net underneath. If using fabric that is not pre-finished, trim off the

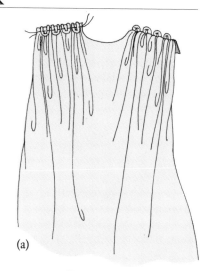

(a)

(b)

selvedges and turn a narrow hem or bind along both long edges and across one end, rounding off the corners neatly.

Fold the train in half at the shoulders and mark the centre. Across the back of the neck the edge of the fabric can be either left straight, scooped out slightly, or draped in a cowl. The remainder is folded into a series of small pleats on each side.

For a straight or scooped neck, mark off 14cm (5$\frac{1}{2}$in) on each side of the centre back. Pleat or gather (or smock) from there to the side edge until each side is 1cm ($\frac{3}{8}$in) shorter than the finished shoulder seam of the dress. Stitch across the pleats to hold. Make four or five rouleau loops to attach to each shoulder edge and stitch to the right side. Scoop out the neckline if you wish by lowering it by 2.5cm (1in) at the centre. Finish the edge by facing it with a strip of lining, net or self fabric (a).

For a cowl neck leave 60 cm (24in) unpleated at the centre, attach the button loops to the *wrong* side and complete by applying a bias strip of satin to the wrong side and finishing it flat on the right side (b).

Sew buttons to the shoulders of the dress to correspond with the loops. Further embellishment can of course be added to the shoulders.

Do not forget to insert weights in the hem of the train. Either sew small lead weights at intervals – the number required will vary according to the fabric used – or insert a length of continuous hem weight. This is a narrow tape containing small lead shot which is often used in curtains.

Remember to practise walking beforehand in order to cope with a train and arrange for a friend – not a bridesmaid – to be waiting in the church doorway to arrange it behind you as you go into the church. Where full trains and hooped or crinoline dresses are involved, it is a good idea to go to the church and walk down the aisle before the day to make sure you can get through without difficulty.

Remember also to look at the overall effect of the veil when combined with the train, before making a final decision on the length of each.

Flounce for train or back of dress

A graded flounce can be gathered along the middle and stitched to the centre back of the dress, or it can be attached to the train. It can be made in single fabric with the outer edge hemmed, or from double fabric, stitching the two together round the outer edge and turning it right side out before gathering. Further alternatives include making it double but using two colours; making it from lace; adding lace to the edges, or putting a narrow lace flounce on top down the centre. Any version can be decorated with beads, pearls, sequins etc. or with any of the decorative techniques.

The measurements given below provide a flounce that is shaped at the hem to correspond with the train hemline on p. 73. If you attach it to a skirt without an extension for a train, trim the lower edge so that the hem follows the shape of the dress hem. In both cases the dress must have the hem length established and the hem turned up and tacked before attaching the flounce even if it has not been finally stitched.

FABRIC   You will need 3m (3$\frac{1}{4}$yd) fabric 75cm (29$\frac{1}{2}$in) wide.

PATTERN   Make a paper pattern following the diagram shown, or fold the fabric lengthwise and mark the shape to be cut out. Cut a rectangle of paper 2m70 (2$\frac{7}{8}$yd) long and 34cm (13$\frac{1}{2}$in) wide. Label one long edge 'Fold of Fabric'. At the bottom, measure up from the right hand corner 34cm (13$\frac{1}{2}$in) and at the top of the rectangle measure 8cm (3$\frac{1}{4}$in) from the left hand corner. Join

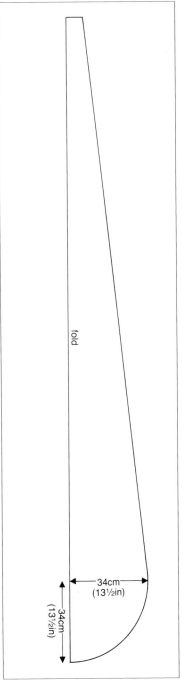

the two points with a straight line. Complete the outline by drawing a curve at the lower edge.

Avoid belt loops for sashes except in small bridesmaids, because they will stick out at the side and be visible to those behind. Instead, either tack sashes in place at the last minute or sew press studs or a couple of Velcro Spot-Ons near the side seams.

CUTTING OUT Cut one piece with pattern to the fold of the fabric, or two if required. Mark the centre for gathering by pressing a crease along the fold. A seam allowance of 1cm (⅜in) is included round the outer edge. The upper edge will be included in the waist seam of the dress. Insert gathering thread along the middle, pin upper edge to right side of dress at waist, pin lower edge to hem. Pull up gathers to fit. Attach by stitching down the centre.

Frill

An alternative decoration for the train is a narrow frill. There is no necessity to cut a paper pattern. Cut the frill as described. You will need 85cm (33in) of 90cm (36in) fabric or 70cm (27in) of 115cm (45in) fabric. From 90cm (36in) fabric, cut six pieces across the width 12.5cm (5in) wide. From 115cm (45in) fabric, cut five pieces.

To curve the ends to fit the train hem, place two pieces of frill together with ends level. Mark a point 12cm (4¾in) along one long edge and draw a curve from there to the corner.

Join all frill pieces end to end. Press joins. Turn a hem round outer edge of frill, taking 1cm (⅜in) seam allowance. Decorate if

desired. Gather frill and attach to train, turning in a narrow hem along each side of train from the end of the frill. Alternatively, the outer edge of the train can be faced; in this way the frill would be enclosed between the two layers.

SHOULDER FRILL FOR PANEL BODICE

Single frill for insertion in bodice panel seams

If shoulder frills are required for more than one dress make a paper pattern, otherwise the shape shown could be drawn directly onto double fabric.

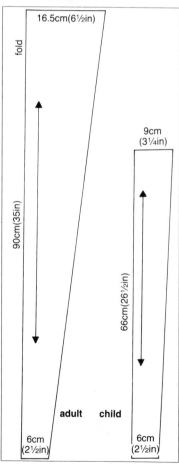

16.5cm(6½in)

fold

90cm(35in)

9cm (3¼in)

66cm(26½in)

adult   child

6cm (2½in)   6cm (2½in)

Rule a vertical line 90cm (36in) long. Rule a horizontal line at the top 16.5cm (6½in) long and write 'FOLD' on the line. At the lower end, which is the waist edge, rule a horizontal line 6cm (2⅜in) long. Complete the pattern by ruling a line at an angle, joining the ends of the horizontal lines. Cut out the pattern.

Place pattern on fabric to the fold and cut two frills in this way. The straight edge is the outer edge to be hemmed; the sloping edge is to be gathered and attached to the bodice. A seam allowance of 1cm (⅜in) is included on the long outer edge. An identical seam allowance is made on gathered edge.

Double frill

Draw the pattern as above on a large piece of paper, but before cutting it fold the paper along the long straight line. Cut out the pattern with paper folded. Open out and cut twice to the fold of the fabric.

A seam allowance of 1.5cm (⅝in) is included all round.

SHOULDER FLOUNCE

Copy the pattern shown onto paper. Rule a vertical line 172.5cm (68in) long and mark it as 'inner edge'. Rule a horizontal line at the top 12.5cm (5in) long; label it 'centre back seam'. At the lower end, rule a line 16.25cm (6½in) long and label it 'centre front – FOLD'. Find the middle of the vertical line and rule a horizontal line. Mark off a point 18.5cm (7¼in) along it for top frill and another at 26.25cm (10¼in) for main frill. Measure down the vertical line 20cm (8in), mark a dot to indicate the point for attaching to strap at bodice edge. Level with this, mark points at 8.75cm (3¼in) and 13.75cm (5½in) for the top and main frills respectively. At the lower end of the vertical, measure up 22.5cm (8¾in) and mark the bodice attachment point. Mark the frill edges at 15cm (6in) and 20cm (8in). Cut out the main frill on double fabric with back edge to fold. Trim pattern and cut upper frill in the same way.

A hem of 1cm (⅜in) is allowed along each outer edge. The same allowance is made on other edges.

To make the flounce fold each piece of fabric with right sides together and with short ends level. Stitch across the end and press the seam. Turn a hem all round outer edge of flounce and press. Finish the elasticated edge either by making a stitched casing or use shirring elastic. To make a casing, fold the edge to the wrong side taking 1.5cm (⅝in) seam, turn under the raw edge, tack and machine stitch on the fold leaving a 1cm (⅜in) gap at the centre back. Thread narrow elastic webbing through the casing and pin the ends together. Pin flounce to dress, matching dots to straps on bodice. Adjust the elastic and stitch the ends together.

To use shirring elastic, finish the neck edge of the flounce with a decorative stitch or edging.

Don't tie a ribbon sash round the waist – it won't stay in place. Instead, stitch it along one edge nearly all the way round, with right side down to right side of dress, on the waistline. Fold ribbon up over the bodice and press.

Insert three rows of shirring, the first one 1cm (⅜in) from the edge and the others the width of the machine foot apart. Pin flounce to bodice. If the shirring needs tightening, add one or two more rows of stitching. See p. 107 for more details of shirring.

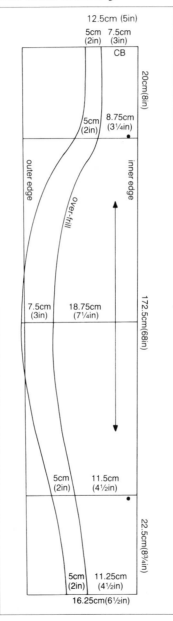

Attach flounce to dress using hand prick stitch and sewing along each side of the elastic casing, or if edge is shirred stitch at the base of the frilled edge just beside the first row of shirring. Alternatively, any decorative hand or machine stitch may be used to attach the flounce: it would have to be unpicked to convert the dress to an off-the-shoulder style. If the flounce is made double, stitch the seams and outer edge of both and then put the narrow flounce wrong side down to the right side of the wider one. Match edges and centre back seams. Make the casing by folding over both edges together or, if using shirring elastic, decorate each edge separately but stitch the elastic through both layers inserting four or five rows instead of three.

SLEEVE WITH SHOULDER CAP

A cap in contrast fabric can be added to the full sleeve, or the cap can be a second layer of the dress fabric. If lace is used, try to have a scalloped edge to correspond with the edge of the cap sleeve. The cap may be made double, perhaps using net or organdie in a contrast colour. The cap sleeve can also be used on its own, in which case gather the sleeve head edge and insert in armhole in the usual way but bind the armhole edge with lining or bias binding to neaten the raw edges. Cut out the dress sleeves, stitch seams, finish hems. Trace or cut off the cap sleeve and cut out on double fabric. Cut again for double caps. Fold cap sleeves right sides together and stitch underarm seams. Turn a narrow hem if required along lower edge and stitch. If caps are double, make the lining sleeves and put right sides together with outer sleeves. Match the seams and stitch round the lower edge taking a 1cm (⅜in) seam. Trim edges, turn so that lining and sleeve are right sides out. Baste together round lower edge and sleeve head. Press.

With dress sleeves right side out, slip cap sleeves over the top right side out and baste together

round sleeve head (below left). Insert gathering thread over sleeve head and attach sleeves to dress. Neaten armhole. Remove tackings.

SLEEVE WITH CENTRE PLEAT OR SLIT

The full sleeve pattern can be cut down the middle and cut out in fabric to allow an inverted pleat which can be decorated to match other features on the dress. Or the sleeve can be split from shoulder to lower edge and worn as it is, or made as an oversleeve in contrasting colour or texture on top of the main sleeve.

Cut the pattern along the central line.

Pleat

Place pattern on double fabric, spreading the pieces and inserting 15cm (6in) between the edges. Pin to fabric and cut out. Mark the

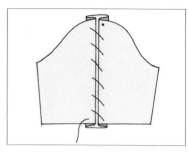

width of the pleat down the sleeves. Work any decoration on the pleat section. Fold fabric on pleat lines, bringing the folds together in the centre. Baste together from hem to sleeve head (above). Stitch sleeve seam, complete hem and attach to dress in the usual way.

Slit

Place pattern on double fabric allowing 1cm (⅜in) seam allowance along each central cut edge of pattern. Cut out. Turn narrow hems along these edges. Press and place edges together at sleeve

---

DRESS DESIGN NO. 4

The panelled bodice with sweetheart neck, sleeve fitted and buttoned from elbow to wrist. The back bodice has a short zip in the centre back seam. The skirt has four panels, probably sufficient for velvet but add more if you wish.

Pattern (see drawings page 121)
PIECES: 2, 3, 4, 5, 6, 7 for
          bodice
          9 for sleeve
          1(A) for skirt

Cutting out

Cut four skirt panels full length, or more in fine fabric. Cut front bodice panel to fold with alternative neckline; mark centre front. Cut out side panels and centre

back panel on double fabric. Cut two sleeves. Cut sufficient bias strip to make eight or ten button loops for each sleeve and six for the cummerbund if used. Cut out neck facings to alternative neckline. Cut facings in Vilene and cut a strip of Vilene 2cm (⅞in) wide for sleeves.

Making up

1. BODICE   Baste or press Vilene to neckline edges. Stitch centre back seam to dot, insert zip in seam. Join side panels to back panel and stitch. Join side front panels to centre front panels. Press seams towards centre. Join back bodice to front at shoulders. Attach facing to neckline. Stitch right bodice seam.

2. SKIRT   Stitch skirt seams, leaving opening for zip at the top of one seam. Turn up and tack hem.

3. WAIST JOIN   Gather skirt and attach to bodice. See p. 54.

4. ZIP   Insert zip. See p. 55.

5. SLEEVES   Attach Vilene to selvedge. Stitch dart opening in sleeve. Make long length of rouleau tubing and make loops for each sleeve. Stitch the loops to the right side of the sleeve on the front edge of the opening. Complete the opening. Turn up hem at wrist or bind. Gather sleeve head. Attach sleeves to bodice. Sew buttons to sleeves. Stitch the hem. Remove all tackings from dress. Press.

VARIATION ON DRESS NO. 4: Traditional bridal features of long fitted sleeves and sweetheart neck emphasised with quilted bodice, hem band and muff.

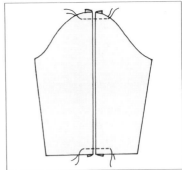

The bodice seams are piped with satin, the sleeves fastened with satin loops and buttons. Work all quilting before cutting exactly to size, adding pearls after the outfit is complete. The hem band can be applied to the four-panel skirt, shaping it to fit or, for a deeper band, cut skirt appropriately shorter, make four quilted sections using lower part of skirt pattern then join each quilted piece to a skirt panel before seaming the skirt

head and hem. Stitch across from one to the other to hold in place (above). Stitch sleeve seam, complete hem and attach to dress in the usual way.

SHOULDER-STRAP HOLDER

For comfort, make strap holders quite long, from armhole to within 1cm (⅜in) of the neckline. Stitch them in position as soon as the shoulder seams are complete. Use a length of rouleau made from lining fabric or else ribbon or stretch lace. Cut two pieces, allowing an extra 2cm (¾in). Turn a 1.5cm (⅝in) hem at one end and stitch round. Sew the knob side of a small press-stud to the end. Place strap holder in position along shoulder seam, turn under the end and hem at the armhole end. Sew the socket part of the press-stud in position.

FITTED BODICE

This is composed of three pieces for the back and three for the front, with a zip in the left seam and facings attached to the upper edge. It may have straps attached, or it may be strapless in which case it must be boned which requires an extra underlining of fabric, lining fabric or soft cotton.

Note that if the figure is full or heavy-busted a boned bodice should be made, still with straps if desired.

Bodice with straps

Cut out all the pattern pieces. Mark centre front and centre back. Stitch front and back panel seams. Stitch right side seam. Press. Make straps by folding fabric right side inside, stitch the long edge. Note that the straps can be made narrower simply by stitching closer to the fold. Trim the raw edges. Turn straps right side out using a rouleau needle; press. Place ends of straps on right side of bodice over the seams and with edges level with the edge of bodice. Baste in place. If possible fit the bodice at this stage and adjust the strap length. Place facings right sides together and stitch the *right* side seam. Press. Neaten outer edge of facing. Place facing right side down on to right side of bodice on top of strap ends. With edges level, tack round upper edge of bodice. Stitch facing to bodice with bodice uppermost to take an even seam allowance all round. Trim edges but not ends of straps unless they have been fitted. Snip shaped edges, turn facing to inside of bodice. Tack round upper edge with straps extending; press. Hold facing down by working hemming or herringbone stitch over the edge of the facing where it crosses the bodice seams. Press. Attach bodice to skirt; insert zip holding ends of facing free of zip, then fold facing down over zip, turn under raw edge and hem to zip tape.

Spread out a sheet on the floor for fittings.

Boned bodice

You will need four pieces of Rigilene polyester boning, two pieces cut to the length of the front bodice edges and two for the back. Stitch panel seams in bodice and stitch right side seam. Press. Stitch panel seams in lining bodice and *left* side seam. Cut lengths of bias lining or bias binding 2.5cm (1in) wide and the length of the bodice seams. Place strips in position over seams on *wrong* side of bodice lining (below). Attach each with two parallel rows of stitching 5mm (¼in) inside raw edge. Tack lining to bodice wrong sides together. Make and attach facings and press as for bodice with straps (bottom).

Insert boning into bias casings. Push boning to the upper edge, mark the point at the waist where the waist join will come, i.e. 1.5cm (⅝in) above the edge of the

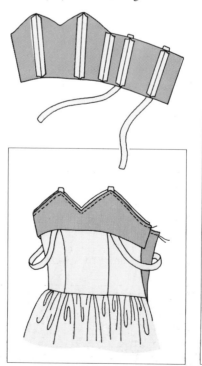

bodice, then *trim each piece of boning 1cm (⅜in) shorter* to allow for movement and for stitching at the waist. Attach bodice to skirt, insert zip. Take care not to press heavily over the boning as it may mark the fabric.

Use a bigger machine stitch than normal, just in case you have to unpick.

CUMMERBUND

A wide stiffened belt covered with pleated fabric, for the adult dresses.

You will need:

One piece of fabric waist measurement plus 8cm (3¼in) and 41cm (16⅛in) wide.

Pelmet Vilene waist plus 5cm (2in) and 10cm (4in) wide.

Thread

10cm (4in) length Velcro or 4 Velcro Spot-Ons.

If you are unable to fit and adjust shoulder strap lengths before facings are attached, stitch across the strap ends at the back with a short row of stitching through bodice strap and facing. Then attach facing by stitching right round bodice in three stages, overlapping the strap stitching by only a few stitches. Then at a later stage, when the dress is fitted and you have to adjust the strap length, simply pull out the short row of stitching, adjust the strap and re-stitch.

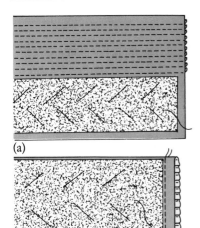

(a)

(b)

Fold and stitch 10 tucks 1cm (⅜in) wide along the length of the fabric between one edge and a point 29.5cm (11⅝in) above the lower edge. Place Vilene on wrong side of fabric with upper edge level with this row of stitching. Make sure seam allowances extend beyond all other edges. Baste Vilene in place (a). Fold fabric *right* sides together, folding it evenly along the edge of the Vilene. With raw edges level stitch along long side and across one short end (b). Turn cummerbund right side out. Press. Turn in open ends to meet each other and slip stitch together. Attach Velcro to fasten.

SASH

A wide fabric sash for adults to tie in a big bow with ends reaching to ankle length.

Cut two pieces of fabric on the straight grain 185cm long and 35cm wide (72in × 14in).

Place pieces right sides together with one pair of ends level and cut at an angle of 45 degrees. Place the other ends level and stitch across the ends to join.

Press join open. Turn a narrow hem all round the outer edge of the sash and machine or hand sew. Alternatively cut 4 pieces of fabric perhaps cutting two in contrast fabric. Join each pair then place them right sides together and stitch round outer edge leaving a gap in one side of 10cm (4in). Trim the raw edges. Turn sash through the gap so that it is right side out. Slip stitch the gap and press.

BELT

A stiffened belt fastened with three rouleau loops and buttons and decorated with any of the motifs or techniques.

You will need:

A piece of fabric 45cm × 90cm (½yd × 1yd)

Pelmet Vilene 10cm × 90cm (4in × 1yd)

Thread

3 buttons (fabric covered)

Cut out a piece of fabric 13cm (5¼in) wide and waist size plus 3cm (1¼in), From the remainder cut a bias strip 10cm (4in) long and 2.5cm (1in) wide. Cut pelmet Vilene to width and shape required.

Make the bias strip into rouleau, cut it into three equal pieces. Place Vilene on wrong side of fabric with one long edge along the middle of the fabric. Baste. Decide where belt will be fastened i.e. centre back, side or

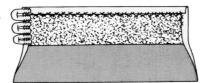

front and work any chosen decoration on the belt so that it will be seen to best effect. Fold narrow raw edge of fabric over on to Vilene along one edge and across both ends. Work herringbone stitch over fabric edges. Fold each piece of rouleau and place all three at one end of the belt on the wrong side, with loops extending. Hem along end of belt and along each side of each loop end to secure firmly. Fold remainder of fabric over the Vilene, baste along the middle of the belt (below left). Trim the outer edge of the fabric until 5mm (¼in) extends. Turn in the raw edge a little more than 5mm (¼in) so that it is hidden from the right side, tack to back of belt and hem along the three sides. On right side sew three buttons to correspond with the loops.

PARASOL

Make a pretty cover for a white or pale-coloured umbrella as follows:

Using plain white or coloured taffeta, cut triangles to fit each section, allowing 5mm (¼in) for the seams along the spokes but up to about 8cm (3in) at the edge. Join sections together with narrow seams for each half of the umbrella. Decorate the seams to co-ordinate with the dress decoration. Join the two halves with one long seam over the top, leaving a space in the centre for the umbrella ferrule. Decorate the seam. Slip the cover over the umbrella, pull it taut, trim the surplus at the edge and oversew it firmly at each spoke. Decorate the edge. Most decoration may be attached using adhesive, but an easy and effective method requiring stitching is to use long strips of net about 6cm (2¼in) wide, with edges folded to the centre and pressed. Gather along the middle, using shirring elastic on the bobbin, then apply it to the fabric using a machine stitch but with the ruched net unstretched. Ribbon can be laid along the middle and the stitching worked through that too. This decoration looks attractive stitched in circles or in a continuous whirl over the parasol starting in the centre. To do this, join all the sections together and draw a line on which to place the net. Stitch net ruching round the edge after putting the cover on the umbrella. Decorate the ferrule and the handle.

COVERED HANGER WITH MATCHING LAVENDER BAG

You will need:

1 wooden hanger

Polyester wadding 45cm × 10cm (17⅞in × 4in)

Fabric 58cm × 12cm (23in × 5in); 12cm × 15cm (4¾in × 6in)

Bias strip of fabric 18cm × 2cm (7in × ¾in)

30cm (12in) of narrow ribbon.

Wrap the wadding round the hanger, overlapping the edges on the top. Hold it in place with large loose oversewing stitches; start at the hook and work out to the end on each side. Fold bias strip right sides together and stitch 6mm (¼in) from the fold.

Turn right side out, using a rouleau needle. Trim the ends and slip the tubing over the hook of the hanger, cut off surplus fabric and neaten the end. Turn in the long edges of the fabric 1cm (⅜in) and press. Fold fabric and press a crease to indicate the centre. Wrap the fabric round the hanger, hold the pressed edges together on the top, hold the centre creases at the hook and work small running stitches from the centre to the end, ruching the fabric and shaping it over the hanger. At the end turn in the edges and continue gathering across the end. Fasten off thread strongly. Gather up the other end in the same way.

To make lavender bag, press a 3cm (1⅛in) hem on each long edge and insert two rows of stitching to form a casing for the ribbon. Cut the ribbon in two and thread a piece through each casing, leaving only 5mm (¼in) extending at one end. Fold the fabric right sides together, stitch across the end with long ribbon ends stopping short of the casing. Stitch the other end right across to catch the ends of the ribbon. Fill bag with lavender, pull up ribbon and knot. Tie on to hanger.

Start by making a temporary padding cover for a coat hanger to keep the dress on while it is being made; foam shoulder pads will do. Then when the dress is almost complete, cover the hanger with ribbon, fabric etc., and make a matching lavender bag. It is nice to make one for each of the bridesmaids too.

MUFF

An accessory for a winter wedding; especially effective made in velvet. Reduce the size slightly for small bridesmaids.

You will need:

Velvet or other fabric: 53cm × 35cm (21in × 13¾in)

A piece of wadding and a piece of plain cotton backing fabric the same size

A piece of lining 53cm × 23cm (21in × 9in)

1m90 (2yds) cord

2 tassels

Pearls or beads or alternatively the bird, butterfly, flowers or rosettes (see p. 90) could be attached

Thread

Place the wadding between the velvet and the backing material with both fabrics right side out. Baste together around outer edge. Mark diagonal lines for quilting 5cm (2in) wide or attach a space bar to your machine and stitch. See p. 98 for further details.

Fold the fabric with right sides inside and stitch the ends together. Press open the seam. Fold the piece of lining in the same way and stitch and press the seam.

With muff right side out, attach beads or pearls where lines of quilting cross, leaving at least 5cm (2in) of fabric free of decoration along both edges.

Turn lining wrong side out and slide it over the muff so that both fabrics are right sides together. Baste round ends with edges level and the main seams matching. Stitch round the ends, leaving a gap in one seam 15cm (6in) long. Trim the raw edges, turn muff right side out. Slip-stitch the opening in the seam. Work the end seams to the inside of the muff where they cannot be seen. Fold the muff so that the main seam is mid-way down one side; this will be the back of the muff. It looks novel if the outer half only is decorated. Add any additional embellishments to the muff.

Thread the cord through the muff and knot the ends, adjusting the length on the bridesmaid concerned. Attach the tassels, sew pearls or beads to the tassel heads.

DOLLY BAG

For bridesmaids of all ages, this bag can be made using small spare pieces of any fabric, even the experimental samples of decoration tried out for the dress.

You will need:

2 decorated panels 20cm × 13cm (8in × 5in). If you haven't any pieces you can use, then decorate a piece of fabric by stitching on rows of lace, ribbon of various widths, different edgings etc., using up any scraps you have that match or tone with the colour scheme.

2 plain panels 20cm × 13cm (8in × 5in)

Lower band 43.5cm × 10cm (17in × 4in)

For base section: cut a circle 16cm (6$\frac{3}{8}$in) in diameter.

2m (2$\frac{1}{4}$yds) ric-rac edging

2m80(3yds) narrow ribbon

Thread

A piece of fabric to line the bag, preferably cotton or something stiff enough to support the bag. Cut one piece 43.5cm × 27cm (17in × 10$\frac{1}{2}$in) and another the same size and shape as the circular base of the bag.

A seam allowance of 1.5cm ($\frac{5}{8}$in) is included.

Place ric-rac braid on right side of decorated panels on the two long edges (a). Stitch along the middle. Join the four panels, alternately plain and decorated, taking care to follow the stitching on the ric-rac. Leave 5mm ($\frac{1}{4}$in) gaps in the stitching 6cm (2$\frac{3}{8}$in) from the upper edge on two opposite seams (b).

Stitch ric-rac braid to right side round upper and lower edges, sewing along the middle of the braid.

Fold lower band of bag right sides together and join the ends. With right sides together stitch band to lower edge of decorated section, following the stitching in the ric-rac. Press seam towards band.

With right sides together, stitch the band to the base.

Make lining by folding main section right sides together and stitching the seam from the base for 10cm (4in). Join base to lining right sides together (c).

Put bag and lining right sides together with top edges level and stitch (d). Turn bag through gap in seam. Slip-stitch the gap and push lining inside bag. Press.

Make two rows of stitching 5mm ($\frac{1}{4}$in) apart, 4.5cm (1$\frac{3}{4}$in) below upper edge to form a channel. Cut the ribbon in two.

Thread one piece through channel; join ends. Thread second piece but using the other opening. Join, and pull through, hiding the joins in the channel.

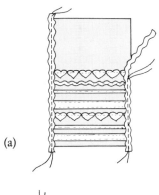

(a)

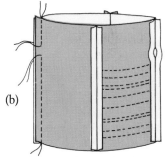

(b)

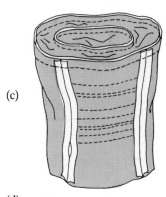

(c)

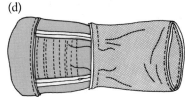

(d)

FLAT CLUTCH BAG

An elegant bag for bride, brides-maid, bride's mother or any of the major guests. Use firm fabric, which may be fabric from the dress or a contrast. Moiré taffeta is effective. A matching pill-box hat or stiffened circlet could be made. Use white, or choose colours to tone with outfit.

You will need:

60cm × 30cm (24in × 12in) main fabric and a piece of lining material the same size.

50cm × 30cm (20in × 12in) pelmet-weight Vilene.

50cm × 50cm (20in × 20in) satin fabric for flowers.

50cm × 25cm (20in × 10in) soft iron-on Vilene.

Thread

A selection of small beads that match and contrast with the fabric, e.g. pearls and silver bugles

3 drop beads for the flower centres

5 feathers to match or tone with the flowers

2 Velcro 'Spot-Ons'.

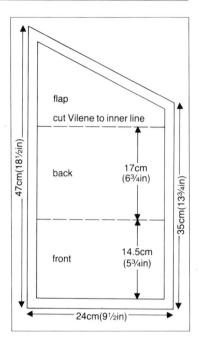

DRESS: DESIGN NO. 5

The fitted bodice and full length tiered skirt with single or double shoulder flounce. The flounce is stitched to the shoulder straps for security but if you wish to wear it off the shoulders later, the straps could be removed.

Alternatively if the wedding dress is made from cotton fabric it could be dyed afterwards, perhaps adding a different flounce. The skirt panels are covered by frills so lining or plain cotton material could be used for the panels.

Pattern (see drawings page 121)

PIECES: 11, 12, 13, 14, 15, 16
         for bodice
         1(D) for skirt plus frills

Cutting Out

Cut out centre front and back panels to fold. Cut side panels on double fabric. Cut out one or two shoulder flounces following instructions on p. 76. Cut facings in Vilene. Cut four skirt panels to appropriate hemline and frills as follows: nine pieces 50.5cm (20in) deep to attach to skirt hem; 7 pieces 48cm (19in) deep to attach to placement line; six pieces 24cm (9½in) deep to insert in waist seam. All frills quoted 90cm (36in) long. Cut straps 60cm (23½in) long and 8cm(3¼in) wide.

Making up

1. BODICE   Make up strapless boned bodice, see p. 79.

2. SKIRT   Stitch skirt panels together leaving seam open below waist for zip. Join together the nine pieces that make up the lower frill, hem the lower edge, gather and attach to lower edge of skirt. Join together the seven pieces that make the middle frill, hem the lower edge, gather and attach to placement line on skirt. Join the six pieces that make the waist frill but leave one seam open where the zip comes. Hem the lower edge of the frill and also the edges of the seam as they will fall on top of the zip. Gather up waist of skirt and stitch to waist tape. See p. 54. Gather waist frill, place on top of skirt with right side up and gathered edges level; stitch together. Join skirt to bodice.

Keep some of the flowers from the bouquet and make them into a pressed flower picture.

VARIATION ON DRESS NO. 5
Filmy voile or point d'esprit is
perfect for this scalloped bride's
or bridesmaid's dress. The double
layer shoulder flounce tops the
fitted bodice and tiered skirt with
peplum. The scallops can be
machine embroidery, they can
be faced with fabric, or
fabric with a scallop
border could be used

Follow the diagram-pattern. A
1.5cm (⅝in) seam allowance is
included. Cut out fabric, lining
and Vilene to the sizes shown.
Score the Vilene along the dotted
lines. With right sides together
stitch fabric and lining together
along the short straight edge.
Press the seam towards the lining.

Place Vilene on wrong side of
fabric, scored side down and with
short edge of Vilene level with the
seam, leaving 1.5cm (⅝in) seam
allowance extending along angled
and long edges. Baste or pin in
place. Fold fabric over edge of
Vilene all round and baste, allowing sufficent ease in the fabric to
enable the bag to fold easily along
the scored lines (below).

Place lining wrong side down
on top of Vilene, with raw edges
extending beyond the bag. Fold
under edges of lining to just
within the edge of the bag. Tack
and slip-hem lining to bag. Fold
bag along scored folds, tack edges

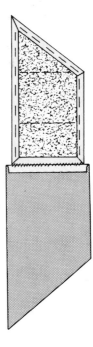

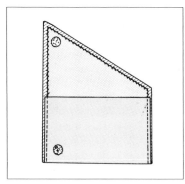

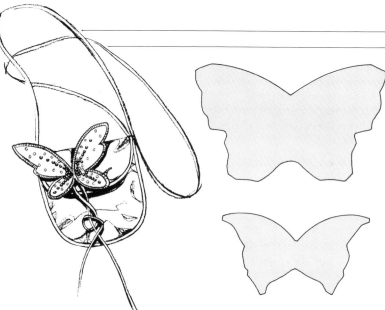

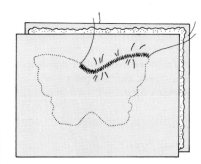

level and machine stitch along each side. Sew the Velcro circles in position under the flap, hemming round the circles by hand.

SHOULDER PURSE

A pretty purse for small brides-maids made in two colours and featuring a beaded, padded butterfly. Use a double layer of crisp fabric such as taffeta.

You will need:

Purse

Main fabric: purse shape as shown in illustration, cut twice. Purse front, lower section shown cut twice.

Contrast fabric: bias strip 2cm (¾in) wide and 2m30 (2½yds) in length

Two pieces of fabric 15cm × 10cm (6in × 4in) and a small piece of wadding for the butterfly

Thread to match both fabrics

Beads

A seam allowance of 5mm (¼in) is included on all edges. Place purse front sections wrong sides together and bind the straight edge using the contrast bias strip.

Place purse sections right sides together, tack round outer edge. Place purse front on top with edges level and tack. Bind round outer edge using contrast bias (below). Make the join in the bias near the fold line of the flap so that it is not too conspicuous.

Butterfly

Outline butterfly (above) on right side of contrast fabric. Tack this to the second piece of contrast wrong sides together with wadding between. Using a small straight stitch, sew round the outline through all layers. Using contrast thread, stitch again covering the straight stitching but using satin stitch set to width 2.

Carefully cut away the surplus fabric, snipping close to the stitching. Add beads; cluster them closely in the centre and space them out over the wings.

Make remaining bias strip into rouleau. Cut off 30cm (12in), fold in half and stitch to the back of the butterfly. Wind one piece

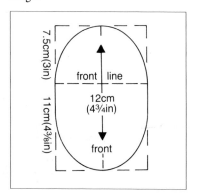

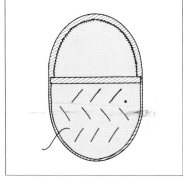

round the other and stitch. Attach butterfly to purse flap.

Use remaining rouleau for strap, turning under ends neatly and hemming to back of purse at the corners.

FLAP BAG

An elegant bag made from any fabric. The front section is separate and the edges are bound. The bag can be made with two front sections if you wish, joined to the first along the upper edge.

You will need:

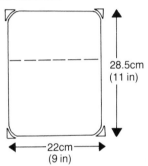

28.5cm (11 in)

22cm (9 in)

The rectangular shape shown in the illustration (above), cut out twice in fabric and once in pelmet-weight Vilene. For the front section, cut four pieces up to the broken line shown on the illustration, and two pieces in pelmet Vilene.

2m10 (2¼yds) bias fabric 2cm (¾in) wide

1 small dome button

Thread to match fabric

There is a 5mm (¼in) seam allowance all round.

Work any stitched decoration on one corner of one piece of fabric.

Make the pieces of front section, putting the Vilene between the layers of fabric, holding along the outer edges with basting tape.

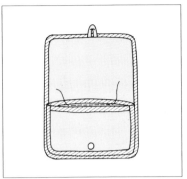

Bind the straight edge of each piece using the bias strip.

Put front sections together with edges level and bind round the outer edge, turning in the strip neatly at the corners.

Make the main section, putting the Vilene between the layers of fabric and binding the outer edge. Join the binding half-way down one side.

Cut 5cm (2in) from the bias and make rouleau. Fold it into a loop and stitch it neatly to the inside of the bound edge in the middle of the flap.

Place front section against bag with outer edges level. Machine the back edge of the section to the bag for a distance of 13cm (5in) (above). Fold flap over and attach button.

Carry your design theme through the whole wedding; use the same bird, butterfly etc., on the wedding cake, printed place cards, napkins and so on.

Take time out to make a garter, a lace-edged handkerchief, a toilet bag; or to embroider initials in blue inside the dress. You will find this relaxing and a welcome break from working on the dress itself.

RING HEADDRESS

Cut two lengths of waistband weight Fold-a-Band to fit your head plus seam allowances. Press the pieces' adhesive sides together. Join the ends by overlapping and zig-zagging. Cut a piece of fabric three times the depth of the ring and long enough to go round it. Wrap the fabric round the ring using basting tape to attach the edge, then turn in and hem the final edge. Twist the fabric so that the seam is inside the ring.

Wind narrow ribbon round and round, pulling it fairly tight. Stitch the ends neatly. This can be decorated with pearls, flowers, butterflies or a bird, or a spray or rouleau or ribbon streamers. It can be worn alone or the bridal veil can be attached. It is especially effective covered in velvet. Decorated with a spray of feathers or flowers or a small veil, it becomes a pretty hat for the bride's mother or for anyone not accustomed to wearing a formal hat.

If you attach a comb to the front to keep on the hat, make sure the comb matches the hair colour and not the fabric as it may be visible.

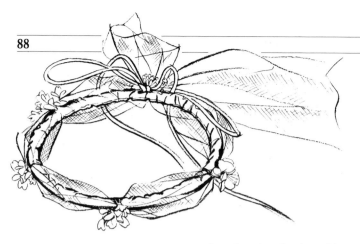

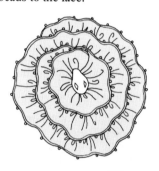

ROSETTES

Use ribbon and wide lace edging. Gather one edge of the ribbon, pulling it up to form a circle. Stitch at the centre to secure, overlap ends of ribbon, turn under raw edge and press. Trim surplus ribbon. Gather the lace edging, but pull it fairly tight at the centre; place in the middle of the ribbon to fill the hole. Secure with a few stitches. Add a drop bead, ball button or ribbon rose to the centre, or add tiny pearls or beads to the lace.

TULLE HEADDRESS

Make a circlet of florist's wire 18cm (7in) in diameter. Cover the wire with wadding, wrapping it round and securing it with large basting stitches. Cover the circlet with fabric. Cut a strip 6cm (2½in) wide and wrap it round, pinning it at the outer edge. Turn under the raw edge round the outside of the circlet and hem down. Twist the fabric cover until the stitching is out of sight along the inner edge. Cut a long piece of soft tulle or veiling 20cm (8in) wide, crush it and stitch it to the fabric at intervals, leaving loops of tulle between. Attach tiny silk flowers (or any of the roses, flowers, butterflies described), covering the stitching; trim the edges of tulle at the back, add flowers and a 1 metre (1yd) length of rouleau made into a spray of loops or a bow.

lace, keeping the thread loose between beads to allow the elastic to stretch. Add a narrow ribbon bow to the garter.

FLOWER HEADDRESS

Make a circlet 18cms (7in) in diameter (smaller for small heads) using 3 strands of florist's wire. Insert small silk flowers as you twist the wire. Add ribbons tied in streamers to the back or loop the ribbon round the circlet between the flowers. Twist all flowers and leaves away from inner edge of circlet.

GARTER

Use 60cm (24in) lace that has a scalloped finish along each edge.

Join the ends with a flat lace join. Using shirring elastic on the bobbin, make three rows of stitching along the centre 5mm (¼in) apart. Sew small beads and bugle beads on the raised gathers of the

COVERED BUTTONS

Cover button moulds with fabric, or send away to have them made, and decorate them. Suggestions (see drawings top right) include:

A tiny ribbon rosebud

A rosette of narrow lace edging or ribbon

Tiny pearls or beads round the edge or covering the button

One drop pearl in the centre

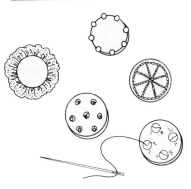

Hand embroidery, gold, silver or coloured French knots are easy to do, as only a small amount of fabric is picked up.

SKULL CAP

Buy a pre-shaped mould; these are usually made from stiff buckram. Cover it by stretching fabric over it, turning the edges to the inside of the cap and oversewing it. Stitch ribbon, binding, lace to the edge. Cover the cap additionally if you wish by adding tiny flowers, beads or any motif. The bridal veil can be attached to the cap; alternatively, make a bow from fabric or tulle or attach ribbons as bows or curly streamers. Sew a small comb to the inside edge at the front.

CUSHION

Make a cushion from the scraps of wedding dress fabrics, repeating the decorative theme or motif.

When covering your own buttons using moulds, e.g. Trims, place a circle of lining under the fabric, put a gathering thread in the edges and dampen the top of the button to make the fabric stick.

To make a single cushion, stitch together two small plain white handkerchiefs, leaving a gap in one side. Stuff well with kapok and stitch up the gap. Cut a piece of fabric the same size as the handkerchiefs and apply the decoration. Make a narrow frill, gather it and apply to the right side all round the edge, taking 5mm ($\frac{1}{4}$in) seam allowance.

Cut a piece of fabric 10cm (4in) longer but the same width as a handkerchief. Turn a narrow hem along each end, cut the fabric in half, reverse the pieces and overlap the hemmed edges at the centre until they equal the size of the other piece of cushion. Pin together at the centre. Place this right side down on right side of frilled piece; tack all round the edge. Turn the fabric over and stitch together following the previous line of stitching. Turn right side out and pull over the stuffed cushion. The cover is made smaller for a well-padded effect.

A larger cushion can also be made, using up the test pieces of decoration that you did. Even unfinished samples will make the cushion a charming memento. Make four cushion pads as above, then make four covers slightly smaller but omit the frilled edging. Cut four pieces for the backs the same size and make each cover by stitching pairs together

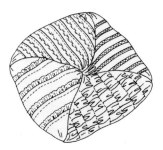

with right sides facing. Leave a gap in the stitching on one side. Turn covers right side out, insert pads and stitch up the gap. Stitch the four cushions together, oversewing the edges neatly. If you have any spare ribbon add a bow to the centre or use up any experimental rosettes, flowers or butterflies.

BUCKLES

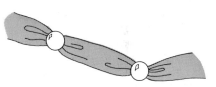

Cover a buckle kit with fabric or have buckles made, omitting the prong. Decorate and attach to shoes, bags, belts, even headdresses and hats. The buckle looks best if first threaded with wide satin ribbon. Even on a belt it is best to use the buckle decoratively at the centre and fasten the belt at the side using Velcro.

Use ribbon that is wider than the buckle, thread it through and mark the parts of the buckle that remain visible. Remove the ribbon and decorate the buckle with any of the following, sewing or sticking them in place:

beads

sequins

lace edging, gathered and attached to outer edges

butterfly

rosette

ribbon roses

narrow ribbon stitched at 1cm
(⅜in) intervals with a bead or a
pearl

Insert the ribbon; neaten the ends
either by inserting in a seam or by
folding under and stitching or
sticking in place. Use adhesive on
shoes and hats; use Wundaweb on
belts etc.

FABRIC FLOWERS, FOLIAGE, BIRDS AND BUTTERFLIES

The flowers, butterflies, roses and
sprays described can be used on
any part of the bride's outfit or on
those of the main participants.
Suggestions for use on or with
other accessories include:

head-dresses
brimmed hats
pillbox hats
bags and dolly bags
purses and shoulder purses
belts
pillows
posies
clutch bags
gloves
shoes
baskets
cummerbunds
photograph album
pin cushions

Suggestions for use on dress
include:

neckline
elbow
back waist
edge of train
shoulder
front waist
looped overskirt
dress hemline

Open flowers

These are made from fabric and
can be sewn singly or in a group to
head-dresses, hats, bags and so on.

You will need, in addition to
the fabric, beads etc. and fuse
wire.

Form five petal shapes using
the wire; cover the shapes by
stretching pieces of coloured
tights over them. Stitch through
the fabric at the base to hold it
taut. To make stamens thread the
beads on to fuse wire, fold wire
and twist beneath bead. Fold
petals round stamens and twist
the ends of wire round the petals.
Sew flower to the centre of a
length of ruched-up lace edging
or nestle it in the centre of some
feathers and stitch in place.

Satin flowers

Make three and attach to the flap
of a clutch bag nestling in feathers
or they can be used on hats,
head-dresses etc.

Trace the petal shape shown and
make a cardboard template (a).
Divide the satin fabric in half and
outline the template on the right
side of one half. Draw five petals
for each flower, all facing in the
same direction.

Press iron-on Vilene to the
wrong side of the remaining half
of the fabric. Place both pieces of
satin together wrong sides
together and baste. Stitch round
all petal outlines with a small
close zig-zag stitch. Carefully trim
round each petal, snipping away
the fabric close to the stitching.

Sew three rows of beads along
each petal, spacing out those at
the end of each row, then thread
a number of varied beads onto the
needle, attaching the end to the
base of the petal (b).

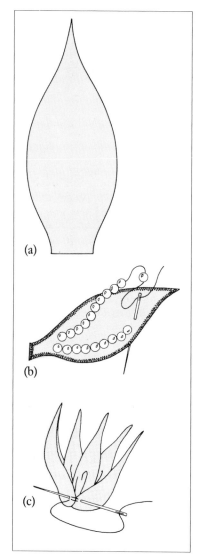

(a)

(b)

(c)

Line up five petals and insert a
running stitch along the edges of
them all. Pull up (c) the thread so
that the petals stand up. Lift each
one and stitch it on the underside
to the next petal, overlapping the
edges. Sew a large bead, pearl or
drop-bead in the centre of the
flower. Arrange three feathers in
half-circles and sew to the bag or
garment, then sew the flower to
the middle.

Ribbon roses

You will need single satin ribbon in white or colours; needle and thread; florist's wire and green tape; leaves you can buy or make.

Cut a length of wire 10cm (4in) long, which can be trimmed later if necessary. Bend over 1cm ($\frac{3}{8}$in) at one end. Slip one end of the ribbon under the wire hook and wind the ribbon round several times. Anchor with a couple of stitches at the base of the ribbon

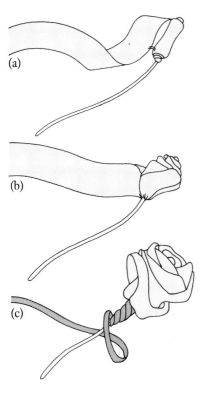

(a)

(b)

(c)

(a). Fold ribbon across at right angles, satin side uppermost, and use the thread again to hold it at the edge. Wrap the ribbon round several times, holding it tightly against the wire at the base; insert a few stitches to secure. This forms the tight centre of the rose (b). Fold the ribbon over at right angles again and wind round the wire. Continue in this way, folding and winding and bringing the base of the rose further down the wire to fan out the top. The bloom can be made as tight or as full as you wish. Wrap green tape round the base and down the wire to finish (c). Join several together, adding leaves if you wish. Ribbon streamers can also be attached.

Remember that colour can be introduced in the middle of the rose, and also that contrast colours of ribbon can be joined back to the back using Wundatrim.

Fabric sprays

A selection of different types of fabric can be used to make flowers and leaves.

You will need, apart from pieces of fabric, florist's wire, thread in various colours, green plastic tape, tiny beads, pearls etc. and copper fuse wire for stamens.

To make transparent flowers with floppy petals, draw a five-petal flower on a soft transparent fabric such as voile, organdie or georgette. Stitch round the outline with a very small zig-zag stitch. Trim the surplus fabric close to the stitching. Thread the fuse wire through the beads, twisting the wire to make stamens 2.5cm (1in) or so long before threading on another bead. Group ten or twelve together and push the ends of wire through the centre of the flower, using a bodkin or stiletto

to pierce a hole if necessary. Put a hairpin or grip through the loops of wire; use the ends of wire to wind round the fabric and hold it close to the stem. Cover the hairpin with green tape.

If machine stitching spoils the appearance of the fabric, for example on velvet, omit the stitching and prevent edges fraying by brushing with Fray-Check liquid.

Alternative flower shapes can be made using heavier fabrics. Cut out small star shapes and make the centres using a bead threaded on to fuse wire and pulled to the under side. Cover with white plastic tape to form a stem. To make leaves outline the shape on fabric with a small close zig-zag. Add the central vein by zig-zagging over the fuse wire. Alternatively, stick two leaves together using fabric adhesive with the wire between the layers, then zig-zag round the leaf.

Flowers and leaves can be stiffened as follows. Into an almost empty bottle of colourless nail varnish, put acetone in the ratio of five or six parts of acetone to one part of varnish. Shake well. Paint the fabric by dabbing on the liquid, using the brush in the bottle. When dry the fabric will be stiff, enabling you to crease the petals etc.

If the bride has not made up her mind about a particular feature – for example depth or fullness of frills, shape of neckline, length of sleeve – make that part from pieces of lining, soft sew-in Vilene or any odd piece of fabric you have. Tack in place for fittings until she makes a final decision.

ROULEAU FLOWERS

A length of rouleau can be arranged in loops to represent petals. Stab-stitch through the centre each time the rouleau is taken across. Make small flowers consisting of seven petals, or much larger ones can be made to represent chrysanthemums. Finish the centre with a pearl, a bugle bead, a tiny lace rosette or a tight swirl of rouleau.

MINIATURE ROSETTES

Use ribbon 5mm (¼in) wide and lace edging a little wider. With edges level, gather along one side pulling up the gathers very tightly. Overlap the ends and secure with a few stitches.

Add petals to the back by folding a length of narrow ribbon to form two mitres 2–3cm (¾–1¼in) apart; secure at the centre, trim the ends of ribbon, then sew the rosette to the middle.

Small rosettes can also be made

from any suitable edgings such as scalloped, embroidered, broderie anglais etc. Fabric can also be used, cutting strips on the straight grain which are the diameter of the finished rosette. Fold the strip down the centre, right side out, and gather the raw edge. Pull up the gathers tightly, overlap the ends turning the upper one under, and secure with several stitches. Cover the centre with a pearl, lace rosette etc.

BEADED SWALLOW

In addition to being used as an applique motif or embroidered outline the swallow can be made independent of a backing and attached to hats, headdresses, shoes, shoulders, bags, muffs etc.

You will need:

A piece of dress fabric or contrast fabric 30cm × 25cm (12in × 10in). Thick wadding 15cm × 25cm (6in × 10in).

Thread

Tiny beads in one or two colours.

Cut the fabric in two. Trace the bird on to greaseproof paper using an embroidery transfer pencil. Reverse the paper on to the right side of one of the pieces of fabric. Place the wadding between the two pieces of fabric with fabric right sides out and baste round outer edge. Stitch round outline through all layers with a small straight stitch. Alter the stitch to a close zig-zag 2mm (3/32in) wide and stitch again along the outline over the straight stitching. Trim away the excess fabric, cutting carefully close to the zig-zag, take care not to snip the stitching.

Sew beads in clusters on head, body and wings. Attach to bags,

muffs etc., with short bar tacks or deep back stitch worked from the under side.

SEQUINNED BUTTERFLY

You will need fabric, pelmet-weight Vilene, some Bondaweb, pearls or beads and white or coloured sequins.

Press Bondaweb to the wrong side of half the fabric, peel off the paper backing and attach the Vilene by pressing again, remember to use a damp cloth each time.

Outline the butterfly. Stitch over the outline, using a medium width close zig-zag. Carefully trim away the surplus fabric. Sew or stick sequins to the wings. Attach the butterfly to the garment by covering the body with pearls or beads and sewing them through the butterfly and the garment. Add antennae, using gold or silver thread. On head-dress, shoes etc., sew beads in place and then use adhesive to attach butterfly. If you want butterflies to be above the surface use wire, or – on the dress – sew a covered button at each point and sew the butterfly to the button.

This section contains a number of especially decorative techniques that can be used on any of the bridal outfits. Select one that complements the theme you have chosen and that you consider suitable for your fabric. Read the instructions to make sure you have the equipment as well as the skill and the time to complete it; then make a trial sample. It is a good idea to try several different techniques before making a final decision. If you decide on something requiring a template, for example bird or butterfly, make at least three templates before you start, putting one of them away as a reserve in case the originals are mislaid.

It has not been possible to give quantities of haberdashery or of lace, beads etc. so buy plenty before you start. With the exception of ribbon, you may not be able to obtain an exact match at short notice.

The techniques have been selected with regard to their particular suitability for the focal point of the basic wedding dress – the front bodice panel – allowing you to decide where else it can be used. Suggestions you might consider are:

back bodice panel
cuffs and sleeve bands
belt and cummerbund
neck facing of blouson bodice
floating skirt panels
edges of frills
collar of bridesmaid's dress
bodice of bridesmaid's dress
cap sleeve of bride's dress
inside inverted pleat of full sleeve
hem band of bride/bridesmaid's dress
head-dresses, caps and hats
bags, muff and purses
bodice of strapless evening dress
bands of the trousseau items

and in some instances the design can be used on the cake too.

REMEMBER: In all cases the decorative stitching is completed before cutting the bodice panel to size. Fit the bodice with a front panel of lining or Vilene tacked in so that you can note any major adjustments. Bodice panel seams can have frills, lace, piping inserted in addition to the decoration on the panel and bows, flowers and so on can be added. If you don't like it or you make a mistake, you can discard it and try again or substitute another technique. On completion, fold the panel, replace the pattern and cut out.

PREPARATION: Cut out a piece of fabric at least 5cm (2in) bigger all round than the bodice panel pattern piece. Mark the centre front with tacking stitches and mark the centre of the panel by tacking across it.

APPLIQUÉ

Suitable for all except transparent fabrics. Subtle effects can be created by avoiding contrasting colours. For instance, use white fabric on ivory; pale cream on buttermilk; and on coloured fabric use a shade paler for the appliqué colour. Add whatever is appropriate in the way of small beads and pearls after the dress is complete. Baste light sew-in Vilene to the back of the panel. Press Bondaweb to the back of the appliqué fabric. Select your motif – bird, flower, butterfly etc. – and outline the number you require on the fabric. Cut out the motifs and arrange them on the panel. When you have decided on suitable positions, peel off the paper backing and press them in place. Stitch over the edge, using satin stitch set at width 2. Stitch antennae, stamens etc. with a small straight stitch. The appliqué colour can be introduced again with piping, frills, long rouleau streamers at the waist and also in the accessories.

> *The bride should practise sitting and kneeling in her dress at fittings, but don't forget to ask her to walk as well – later with veil and train – to make sure none of it drags off.*

BEADING

Suitable for any fabric. Baste the fabric to light sew-in Vilene. Outline the motif on the fabric. Stitch along all lines with back stitch. Use beads of varying size and colour and sequins where appropriate to outline and fill in the motif, using transparent thread.

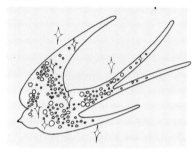

The motif can be thrown into relief by padding it with a small amount of wadding inserted through a slit in the Vilene; this should be done after the motif has been outlined with beads or stitching.

CORDED PIN TUCKS

Suitable for most plain fabrics. Draw diagonal lines across the panel from corner to corner. Insert a wide space twin needle and two reels of matching thread; use a large size straight stitch. Pad the tucks with size 3 crochet cot-

ton, feeding the end up through the hole in the machine plate that is in front of the needle hole. Pull the yarn under the foot towards the back and have the remainder running free on the floor. If your machine hasn't this extra hole, feed it through the needle hole, but then make sure you confine the tucks to straight lines. Very effective patterns of all types can be made with the twin needle. Stitch on the marked lines, then continue making parallel tucks using the foot to space them evenly, until you have the design you want. An attractive hem band can be made using fabric that has been tucked horizontally in this way. A pretty ruched effect can be produced by pulling up the cord in parallel tucks.

VARIATION ON DRESS NO. 6: The modern bride or bridesmaid or even guest wearing a stylish flouncy dress belted and frilled and sharp accessories that are detailed but easy to make. The dress shows the V-neck blouson bodice, short sleeves with bands, four panel mid-calf skirt with flounce. Bag, belt, hat and spray are made from the dress fabric

DÉCOUPÉ WORK

This is suitable for all fabrics and because it uses contrasts in texture as well as weight, some lovely effects can be achieved. Try net with satin, possibly with several layers of net in various colours; satin with velvet; broderie anglais with plain fabric; or, on sleeves or bridal veil, reverse the effect by using satin with net. There are many possibilities.

Select a motif – bird, butterfly, spray of flowers or leaves – and outline it on Stitch 'n' Tear embroidery paper. Baste the fabric to the net, baste the Stitch 'n' Tear to the wrong side. Stitch round the outline with a straight stitch and tear away the design. With right side up, cut away the

top fabric where it has to be removed. Work satin stitch set at width 2½–3 and outline the design stitching over the straight stitching. Use matching thread throughout. Add veins, antennae,

stamens etc. The remainder of the backing fabric can be trimmed away if you wish, but in many cases it is best to leave it as support for the area. Add any beads etc. after the dress is complete.

DRESS: DESIGN NO. 6

The V-neck bodice with short sleeves with band cuffs, the V-neck is a double band of fabric. The skirt is made up of four panels, or more if you wish, with deep hemline frill. The facing and sleeve bands can be decorated. You can make a matching belt or cummerbund. Work the decoration before cutting pieces exactly to size.

Pattern (see drawings page 122)
PIECES: 17, 18, 19, 20 for
           bodice
           8(F) for sleeve
           1(E) for skirt

Cutting out

Cut out back and front bodice to fold. Cut two sleeves. Cut two sleeve bands by measuring soft

Fold-a-Band round the upper arm. Add two seam allowances and cut to length. Use this as a guide, adding seam allowances along both long edges when cutting out the fabric. Cut two back neckbands and two front neckbands. Cut out four skirt panels to length. Cut nine (or seven if fabric is bulky) frills 33.5cm (13¼in) deep in 90cm (36in) fabric or eight (six) if using 115cm (45in) fabric. Cut out facings in Vilene.

Making up

1. BODICE   Stitch front darts. Stitch shoulder seams to dot, snip seam allowances to stitching, turn right side out and complete seam. Make and attach neck facings. See p. 33. Stitch right bodice seam.

2. SKIRT   Join skirt panels, leaving top of one seam open at waist for zip. Join frill sections. Make hem along one edge of frill. Gather frill and attach skirt.

3. WAIST   Gather skirt and attach to bodice (see p. 54). Insert zip in side seam (see p. 55).

4. SLEEVES   Fold bands right sides together, stitch across ends; press joins open. Fold right side out and press. Stitch sleeve seams. Gather lower edge of sleeve and attach to band. Gather sleeve head. Attach sleeves to bodice. Remove all tackings and press.

Tip for the bride: Make sure a sewing machine is on your wedding list.

EDGED TUCKS

Suitable for any type of fabric but particularly easy to do on striped fabric. The 5cm (2in) allowance on both sides of the panel will allow for two pairs of 1cm (⅜in) tucks. If you require more, cut the panel wider. Fold and press the first tuck 3cm (1¼in) from the centre front. Stitch 1cm (⅜in) from the fold and press towards the side. Make another tuck 3cm (1in) from the first and press; make a corresponding pair of tucks the other side of the centre front.

Add machine embroidered scallops to the edge of each tuck (below), putting paper underneath

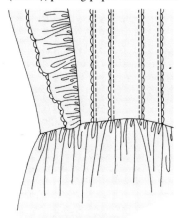

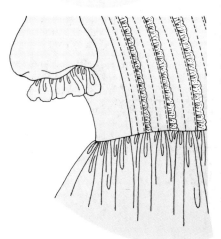

which is torn away afterwards. Alternatively ric-rac braid or lace (bottom left) can be tucked underneath and stitched in place or – for a ruffled effect – make more than two pairs of tucks and stitch gathered lace edging underneath. All these edgings are very effective when used on frills, necklines, sleeve hems etc.

EMBROIDERED MOTIF

Suitable for any plain firm fabric. Use gold or silver thread, Anchor Stranded embroidery threads and tiny pearls or crystal beads. Press or baste light-weight Vilene to the wrong side of the panel. Select the motif – butterfly, bird, flower – and trace it onto greaseproof paper. If you propose having more than one, make copies in paper and arrange them on the fabric to establish the position of each. Outline each motif on the fabric, using small tacking stitches or marking out with dots using a fabric pen. Stitch the outline, using two strands of thread and stem stitch or chain stitch in the same colour as the fabric. Create a shadow effect by adding a line of stitching in gold or silver thread inside all the upper lines. Stitch stamens, veins, antennae etc. in gold or silver; add seeding for dense areas. Make up the dress and add pearls or crystals after it is complete.

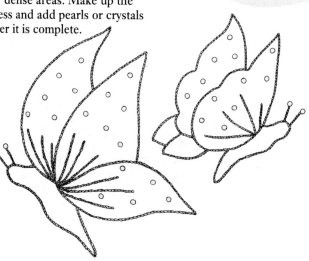

EYELET LACE EDGING

Suitable for all plain fabrics. Thread contrast satin ribbon through the lace and tack to the panel in horizontal rows. Position the top row with the upper edge 1.5cm (⅝in) from the waist edge. Attach in one of two ways: either place the lace right side down, stitch close to the edge of the decoration and fold over and press so that it is right side up; or, turn in the raw edge of the lace and attach with either a straight stitch concealed in the lace, or a decorative machine embroidery stitch in a contrast colour. Fabric frills can be inserted in the panel seams when making up, or use more lace edging.

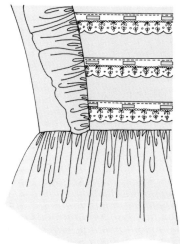

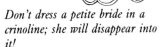
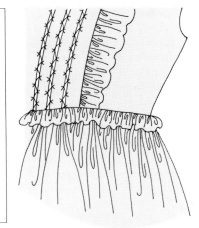

Use iron-on Vilene as interfacing, making sure neck edges and hems are crisp. If the fabric is already stiff, try out several weights of Vilene and several layers on spare fabric until you have the required stiffness.

Use Coats' stretch lace to neaten bodice and waist seams without adding bulk. It could be a way of adding 'something blue' inside the dress.

Don't dress a petite bride in a crinoline; she will disappear into it!

LACE RUFFLES

Suitable for any fabric. Cut the bodice panel much deeper than pattern. Each row of lace takes about 1cm ($\frac{3}{8}$in) of fabric. You can space the rows as you wish, but they are most effective with no more than 3cm ($1\frac{1}{8}$in) (below) between the rows. You will need plenty of narrow lace edging gathered up ready to use.

Begin on the horizontal line across the centre of the panel. Fold the fabric right sides together and press the crease. Open it out and tack the gathered lace on the right side with the edge on the crease. Fold fabric again and tack through both layers and the lace. Stitch on the wrong side parallel with the fold and at sufficient distance from it to allow the lace to extend as far as you would like. Press the fold on the wrong side, but do not flatten the lace. Make the second and subsequent folds by measuring an even distance from the stitching. This distance can be from 1–3cms ($\frac{3}{8}$–$1\frac{1}{8}$in). On completion press carefully on the right side so that all lace lies in the same direction.

EYELET OR FAGGOT-TING INSERTION

Especially suitable for voile, broderie anglais and other cotton and polyester/cottons. Mark three vertical lines on the panel each side of the centre front. Cut the fabric on the centre front line, turn in 5mm ($\frac{1}{4}$in) and press. To attach eyelet insertion, place each fabric edge on the lace against the decorated part; tack and machine using a straight stitch a short distance from the fold to create a tuck or stitch on the edge or over

it using a machine embroidery stitch. An alternative is to put narrow ribbon close to the fold and stitch through the ribbon, the fabric and the lace.

To insert faggotting, finish the edge of the fabric with a straight or decorative machine stitch or with a row of hand-worked feather stitching. Press the edges, then tack them to paper an even 3mm ($\frac{1}{8}$in) apart. The easiest way to do this accurately is to first rule parallel lines on the paper. Work faggotting between the edges. Repeat the technique on all the vertical lines.

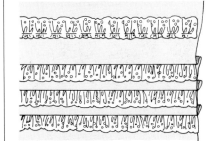

Consider making the top and skirt separately, with a sash or cummerbund to go over the top. This is easier to fit and make up and the skirt can have an elastic waist which will cope with any loss of weight.

Use only white tacking thread; colours will leave marks. This is probably not actual dye that comes out, but even a few hairs from the coloured thread will show up as coloured dots.

If your machine only does a straight stitch, either arrange to borrow one that zig-zags or else hand over the pieces after you have cut out so that they can be zig-zagged all round to neaten the edges.

After it's all over, pack away the dress in black tissue paper (to prevent light penetrating); make a white cotton bag from something like bleached calico and sew the dress into it.

LATTICE EFFECT RIBBON

Suitable for all fabrics except transparent. Use double-satin ribbon 5mm (¼in) wide. With a fabric pen, draw a diagonal dotted line through the centre point of the panel, spacing out the dots 4cm (1⅝in) apart. Mark out more lines on each side to cover the panel, making sure the dots form horizontal lines. Working horizontally and starting at the right, anchor the end of the ribbon on top of a dot with a couple of stitches, using thread to match the ribbon. Laying the ribbon flat, take it diagonally up to the next line of dots and secure on the dot with a pin. Put the needle under the fabric, bringing it up half-way to the pin. Take a stitch round the ribbon, pulling tight to ruche it, slip a tiny pearl on to the needle and take another stitch but this time through the fabric. Pass the needle under the fabric, bring it up at the pin, ruche the ribbon and sew on a pearl. Turn the ribbon and lay it diagonally towards the row of dots below and ruche and stitch it in the same way. Continue like this across the panel. Stitch the second row so that the ribbon forms diamonds. If you use two colours of ribbon attach the ribbon in diagonal lines, using the colours alternately.

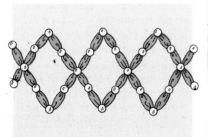

This decoration can be used as described on cuffs, belts and so on; also with the ribbon placed in a straight line as an edging for frills etc.

MACHINE QUILTING

Suitable for all except transparent fabrics, but especially effective on velvet. Place the panel on a layer of thin wadding with a piece of lining beneath. Cover the area with diagonal lines 2.5cm (1in) apart. Do this by marking the lining with fabric pen, then tacking along the lines through all layers; or attach a quilting bar to the machine set at a distance of 2.5cm (1in) from the needle, mark the first line only with tacking, then use the bar. Use a medium-to-large stitch on velvet and sew all lines in the same direction, with the pile, from waist to neck.

Replace the pattern and cut the panel to size. Add tiny pearls to the quilting (below), taking the needle through the wadding between pearls. Satin piping in the panel and waist seams complements the pearls and provides a contrast in texture.

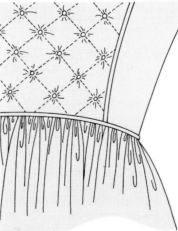

MOCK SMOCKING

A quick and effective decoration worked on the right side of the fabric. It is especially suitable for fabrics with spots or a small square design. If plain fabric is used, begin by using a fabric pen to mark it with rows of dots. Dots should be evenly spaced 5mm–1cm (¼–⅜in) apart.

Begin at the right, using two strands of Anchor Stranded embroidery thread in matching or pale contrast colour. Pick up the first spot, dot or corner of square and also the third in the top row and draw them together with two stitches. Pass the needle under the fabric, slotting it into the fold made by the stitches, and bring out at the dot below. Join this dot to the next alternate dot with two stitches. Pass the needle back to the row above and join the next two alternate dots. Continue in this way, working along two rows of dots, then move down to the next two rows and so on until you have the required effect.

Note that if the fabric has spots that are arranged alternately, either limit the smocking to two rows only or miss out two spots and rows each time instead of one of each. This creates a much bigger design.

> Make the waist join of the dress firm. There is a lot of strain on it due to the weight of the skirt. The waist seam can be piped, can have narrow ribbon stitched on top or can be stitched twice for strength. If you have to unpick part of it to make an alteration, play safe and re-stitch the entire waistline.

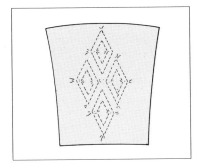

MOTIF QUILTING

Suitable for all plain fabrics and can also be used if the fabric has a geometric design on it. Baste a thin layer of polyester wadding to the wrong side of the panel. Select and mark out a design on soft sew-in Vilene and baste it to the wadding. Use a medium straight stitch and matching thread. Stitch round the design. Carefully pull all thread ends to the wrong side so that there is no overlapping of stitches, and tie.

PAINTING

You can decorate your wedding dress quite beautifully by scattering some hand-painted butterflies or a flight of swallows around a hem, all over tiny puffed sleeves, around the neckline or on a cummerbund. The possibilities are just as varied as with any of the other decorative techniques, and

can be combined very happily with them: you could, for example, apply beading to a swallow for eyes and other details.

Obviously any painting, whether on paper or fabric, requires experience to carry it off well, but the simplest method – and the one that is safest – is a form of printing, which will allow you to practise first on a spare piece of material so as not to risk making mistakes on the finished garment. Screen printing is the most efficient, but a little equipment is required. (Selectasine, of Bulstrode Street, London W1, are good specialist suppliers). Block printing is another suitable method, and here all you need is a piece of wood on which your design is cut out.

Stencilling is a relatively simple and very effective form of hand painting. Here you must first of all decide on your subject (let us say in this case that it's a swallow) and make a simple *outline* drawing. Don't worry about details like feathers at this stage, because it's the silhouette that counts. Draw the outline (see below) on a piece of paper – stencil paper is ideal if you have it, otherwise card or even strong brown paper will do, although with use the edges break down, causing the outline to lose sharpness. Leave plenty of clear space around your drawing so that

when painting you don't inadvertently get paint on parts of the dress where you don't want it. Next cut out the drawing carefully; you're now left with a negative impression. Then, having decided exactly where you want to place your motif or motifs, do a few experimental ones on a spare piece of material to get the feel of the consistency of the paint against the texture of the dress fabric. If the paint is too liquid it will flood, so these preliminaries are important for getting the correct feel of your materials.

Dylon make a special fabric paint called Color-fun and you can use this directly onto the dress material. It gives a permanent colour, which can be thinned down with water for a softer tone, or mixed with other colours (there are twelve in the range) exactly as you would ordinary acrylics.

When you are ready to begin, place the stencil outline of your swallow or other motif where you want it and stamp it with a stencil brush loaded with your chosen paint colour. When you have finished stencilling your drawings you can further decorate the basic design with hand painting – either by adding, say, flowers, or setting your birds in a background of clouds. Again experiment and practice are the keywords.

The more skilled and adventurous among us can look at other printing methods in specialized books. But remember, if stencilling, painting or printing onto a finished garment, protect the under-layer with a piece of polythene to prevent the design coming through. With something like a sleeve or cummerbund, painting should of course be done before making up the garment.

DRESS: DESIGN NO. 7

The plain bodice with elbow length sleeves and skirt of eight floating panels made in a see-through fabric. The underdress is made from the fitted bodice with six-panel calf length skirt. The sleeves have elastic in the hems, the slash neckline is bound and the dress fastens on the shoulder with five small buttons and rouleau loops made from contrast fabric or fabric of underdress. The waistline is elasticated.

Pattern (see drawings page 122)

PIECES: 11, 12, 13, 14, 15, 16
      for fitted bodice
      1(C) for skirt; 1(D) for
      floating panels
      17, 18, 8(C)

Cutting out

Cut out underdress. Cut back and front centre panels of fitted bodice to fold; cut side panels on double fabric. Cut two pieces of fabric on the straight grain 2.5cm (1in) wide and 58cm (22in) long, to be trimmed to length at fitting. Cut six skirt panels to length. Cut a length of bias fabric 3cm (1¼in) wide and 110cm (43in) long for binding and loops. Cut out overdress. Cut back and front blouson to fold following slash neckline. Cut two sleeves. Cut eight skirt panels to length. Mark centre front and centre back of bodice.

Plan – and practise – your wedding-day hair-style with the dress and – in the final stages – with the head-dress and veil. Don't mix long flowing hair or a natural-dried perm with a sculptured classic dress.

Making up

UNDERDRESS Follow instructions on p. 79 for bodice, and p. 104 for skirt, cutting skirt panels to required length.

OVERDRESS
NECKLINE Stitch right shoulder seam. Press. Make a length of rouleau and space out five loops onto the *wrong* side of the left front shoulder. Fold remainder of bias strip down the middle, right side out, and press. Bind neckline and both shoulder edges with double bias, stitching it to the *wrong* side on top of the loops (below). Take 1.5cm (⅝in) seam allowance on the bodice, but 5mm

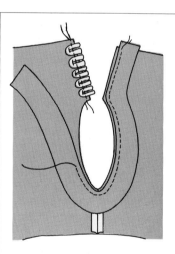

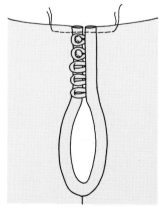

(¼in) only on bias. See p. 26. Finish bias on right side of bodice, using plain or decorative stitching. Put shoulder edges together and stitch across with armholes level (bottom left).

2. DARTS AND SEAMS Stitch darts in front bodice. Stitch both side seams.

3. SLEEVES Stitch seams. Turn a 2cm (¾in) hem and insert elastic to size. Attach sleeves to armholes.

4. SKIRT Hem the lower edge and both long edges of all the floating panels. Join panels together edge to edge at waist by stitching across the top. Insert a gathering thread across the top of each panel. Gather up panels and attach to bodice. Neaten waist join. Stitch buttons to back shoulder. Remove all tackings from dress. Press. Cut elastic to fit waist and attach to seam allowances of waist join.

Use a synthetic thread such as Coats' Drima for all fabrics. It is strong and fine with a lot of give in it, so seams will wrinkle less.

Use white or transparent plastic press studs instead of metal ones.

Keep the partly made dress and all the pieces of fabric wrapped in a cotton sheet; then there will be no static to attract dust.

If the dress is a crinoline, check that the light isn't going to shine straight through it when the bride stands in the sunlight in the church porch.

For bride or special guest, chiffon or voile overdress with sprays of satin ribbon roses at the waist and for the headdress. Underneath, matching or contrast dress with fitted bodice. Boat neck bodice has satin bound neckline and loops and buttons on one shoulder; elbow length sleeves have elastic in the hems; the six panel skirt has eight floating panels over the top. Panel edges and dress hem can be rolled or shell stitched by hand or machine

Try not to panic if you encounter a problem with the dress; consult someone else or ask around for help. Even if you are very experienced you may lose your nerve over this project and it is possible to be so weighed down by the responsibility of it all that you are blind to even simple solutions.

PIN TUCKS

Suitable for all firm fabrics. Work the tucks before cutting the fabric, as there is no accurate way of calculating how much material they will use. Begin at the centre front and fold and press a crease 5mm (¼in) from the centre line. Edge-stitch the tuck and press it. Make another tuck an equal distance the other side of the centre line. Press them to face towards the side edges. Continue to make tucks 1cm (⅜in) apart until you have an area from which you can cut the panel or until you have enough to form a centre section about 10cm (4in) wide.

The Edwardian look can be emphasized by inserting cotton lace in the panel; by inserting lace, or lace-over-fabric frills in the seams and over the shoulders; by making a tucked cummerbund, by sewing small pearls or buttons along the centre front line and by using the sweetheart neckline but putting a small piece of lace behind it.

QUICK APPLIQUÉ

Lovely effects can be quickly created by using Bondaweb to apply lace motifs. No stitching is

needed, although if you wish you can zig-zag or loop-stitch round afterwards. Select suitable parts of the lace fabric and cut out, allowing 3mm (⅛in) all round. Press Bondaweb to the wrong side, putting the lace on greaseproof paper first so that it does not stick to the ironing board. Use a medium-hot iron and damp muslin for pressing and allow the fabric to cool before peeling off the paper backing. Place the motif (with Bondaweb side down) onto fabric and press again. Use the greaseproof paper again if you are putting the motifs on net, chiffon or other transparent fabrics. This method of appliqué is a good choice if you have a lot of decorating to do round the hemlines and so on. Additional decoration can be added in the form of beads.

QUILTED MOTIF

A method of embellishing brocade or printed fabric. It may be suitable for geometric and floral designs depending on the material being used. Not suitable for transparent fabrics.

Select the motif or motifs to be outlined and baste a thin piece of

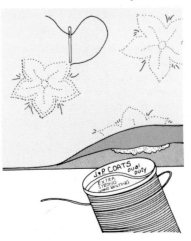

wadding to the wrong side. Baste a piece of lining fabric or lawn over the wadding. When quilting several motifs or perhaps the entire panel, cover the whole area with wadding and lining. Outline the motif with running stitch, using matching thread or gold or silver thread. Highlight any feature or central point with running stitch and add clusters of beads or pearls where appropriate. Cut away the surplus wadding and lining on the backs of single motifs. If the entire panel has been quilted the padding can be left in place, depending on the effect you require.

RANDOM STITCHING

Suitable for all firm plain fabrics, but try it on net too. Stretch the fabric taut in an embroidery hoop. Remove the machine foot and drop the feed teeth. The stitching can be worked from the right or the wrong side; your choice will depend on the thread you use. Matching or contrast sewing thread such as Drima is used on top and underneath; stitch from the right side. Fine gold and silver thread can be used on top with sewing thread underneath; stitch from the right side, but loosen the top tension by two divisions. Heavier contrast or gold or silver thread must be wound on to the bobbin, so stitch from the wrong side loosening the bottom tension.

Remember to lower the lever even though there is no foot. Stitch, wriggling the frame until the entire panel is covered.

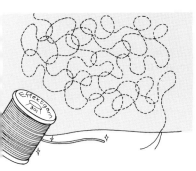

Do not forget to raise the teeth, attach the foot and restore the tension afterwards.

This decoration slightly stiffens the fabric and so is extremely effective on hats, bags, wide sashes, big bows etc.

Narrow ribbons on head-dresses and waists can be curled by running your scissors along them.

RIBBON EMBROIDERY

Suitable for firm fabrics. Press or baste the panel to soft Vilene. Mark out a design on the fabric. Either use fabric pen or draw the design on greaseproof paper, using an embroidery pencil, and press it to the fabric to transfer the outline. Begin at an unobtrusive point or where ends can be neatly overlapped and stitch very narrow ribbon to the outline. Use a small straight stitch and attach the quilting foot for a clearer view. The ribbon curls up attractively, so do not press afterwards.

For a very pretty alternative, use narrow lace instead of ribbon. The lace could be gathered up first.

Remove all tackings before you press; otherwise they will leave marks that are impossible to remove from some fabrics. The slightest pressure on zips, press studs etc. will also leave permanent marks on most bridal fabrics.

RIBBON LATTICE

An effective decoration for plain satin, using narrow satin ribbons of varying widths. For a flat effect press light iron-on Vilene to the wrong side of the panel. Rule parallel diagonal dotted lines over the entire panel. Apply the ribbon to the lines in alternate directions, using the different widths of ribbon in sequence. The ribbon can be stitched down the middle or along each edge; or it can be attached using Wundatrim.

The flat effect of this decoration can be offset by stitching ruched wide lace over the panel seams after the bodice is complete, taking the lace over the shoulder and down the back panel seam, also stitching a line of ribbon down the middle to cover the gathering stitches.

Ribbon weaving can be used to decorate the cake. Decide on the size and shape of a panel or panels and construct by mounting the ribbon on to iron-on Vilene as described for the dress. Trim the panels and place on the cake. Add piped icing round the panel to cover the edges.

Decorate the cake pillars with ribbon too, winding it diagonally and securing the ends with icing.

RIBBON WEAVING

A suitable decoration for all fabrics. Select two or three different types of ribbon the same width – for example, velvet, jacquard and satin all 1–1.5cm ($\frac{3}{8}$–$\frac{5}{8}$in) wide. The ribbon can be white, or colours can be introduced. Cut a piece of soft iron-on Vilene 5cm (2in) bigger all round than the bodice panel. Cut the ribbons into lengths, then arrange them in a plain or twill sequence, weaving them over and under to obtain a pattern – pleasant optical illusions can be created. Having worked out a sequence, arrange the ribbons together with ends level on the Vilene. Press the ends to the edge of the Vilene along the top and down one side by touching with the iron. Having anchored the ribbon, weave them into the design. Press carefully all over to attach to the Vilene. Put the pattern on the weaving and stitch round the outer edge of the panel; cut out just outside the stitching. Use the fabric panel as a lining for the ribbon area.

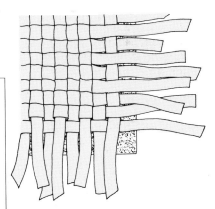

DRESS: DESIGN NO. 8

Full-length strapless petticoat or evening dress from fitted bodice pattern with a skirt made of six panels or more or less if you wish.

Pattern (see drawings page 122)

PIECES: 11, 12, 13, 14, 15, 16, 29, 30 for bodice
1(A) for skirt

Cutting out

Cut out centre back and centre front bodice panels to fold; cut all side panel pieces on double fabric. Cut front and back facings to fold. Cut six skirt panels. Cut out facings in Vilene. Cut out pieces 11, 12, 13, 14 and 1(A) in lining fabric. Cut four bias strips 2cm (¾in) wide for boning.

Making up

1. BODICE   Make strapless bodice (see p. 79).

2. SKIRT   Join skirt sections; join lining sections, leaving a gap for the zip at the top of one seam. Put lining inside skirt with wrong sides together. Match waist and zip edges. Baste together. Gather skirt and attach to bodice excluding bodice lining. Stitch waist seam, neaten join by turning under and hemming the bodice lining to the skirt lining, just covering the raw edges of the seam.

Machine-baste all skirt seams; hand basting won't stand the strain of fitting.

VARIATION ON DRESS NO. 8: Romantic evening dress, fitted, boned strapless bodice with six panel skirt. Centre panel can be contrast fabric or tucks or criss-cross ribbon

3. ZIP   Insert zip in left seam, holding bodice facing clear. Fold facing down into position on inside of bodice, turn under side edges and hem to zip tape. Sew a small hook and thread loop above the zip.

4. HEM   Turn up and stitch dress hem. Turn up lining hem 2.5cm (1in) shorter than dress. Remove all tackings from dress and press.

DRESS: DESIGN NO. 9

Fitted bodice with three-tiered short skirt that can be made as an underdress or as a sundress. It could be made in cotton material for the wedding and dyed for later use.

Pattern (see drawings page 122)

PIECES: 11, 12, 13, 14, 15, 16
             for bodice
             1(E) for skirt plus frills

Cutting out

Cut out centre front and centre back bodice panels to fold. Cut side panels on double fabric. Cut four skirt panels to appropriate length. Cut frills as follows: nine pieces 33.5cm (13¼in) deep to join to lower edge of skirt; seven pieces 27.5cm (10¾in) deep to stitch to placement line on skirt; six pieces 24cm (9½in) deep to insert in waist seam. All frills quoted as 90cm (36in) long. Cut two pieces of fabric 55cm × 4.5cm (22in × 1¾in) on the straight grain for straps. Cut facings in Vilene.

Making up

1. BODICE   Make fitted bodice with straps as described on p. 79.

2. SKIRT   Join frills and attach to skirt, attach skirt to bodice as described for design No. 5. Remove all tackings and press.

*VARIATION ON DRESS NO. 9
This simple strappy dress for bride or bridesmaid would look delightful in plain cotton. The centre panel of the fitted bodice has broderie anglaise edging inserted into inverted tucks; the same edging is in the waist join and applied to the edges of the tiered skirt. Make the straps double length to tie on the shoulders; stitch through the knot for security*

ROULEAU SWIRLS

Suitable for soft fabrics. Press light iron-on Vilene to the wrong side of the panel. Decide where the swirls are to go and mark the centres. Make long pieces of rouleau filled with cord. Stitch the rouleau to the design, starting in the middle and winding the rouleau round and round. Stitch either with slip-stitch under the rouleau; or work from the underside, in which case the design points should be transferred to the Vilene – you can feel the rouleau underneath as you back-stitch through the fabric. If possible, take the end of the rouleau into a seam, or tuck it neatly out of sight, or else finish with a bead or ball button. When used on cuffs the end can be made into a button loop. Finish the centres of the swirls with beads, ball buttons or ribbon rose buds.

If you want to put a little rouleau loop in an edge that has no seam, make a hole in the fold using a stiletto or small knitting needle eased gently between the fibres. Stitch the ends of the loop neatly to the interfacing on the inside.

SHADOW APPLIQUÉ

Use on fine or transparent fabrics. Use either the same material or one that contrasts effectively when placed underneath. The contrast can be slightly stiffer than the main fabric. Cut a piece of appliqué fabric and put it beneath the panel, baste together. Select the motifs and decide with the use of templates where they should be placed. Outline the motifs on the appliqué fabric. Stitch along the outlines; this may be done by hand using herringbone stitch

worked right across the motif, or by machine using a small straight stitch. Thread can match the main fabric or it could be gold or silver. Alternatively, the design can be marked on the upper side and outlined with back stitch or – by machine – using a narrow space twin needle. On the underside carefully cut away the contrast fabric round each motif, trimming close to the stitching. Alternatively, you may prefer to cut away the fabric within each motif. This decoration is very effective on full sleeves.

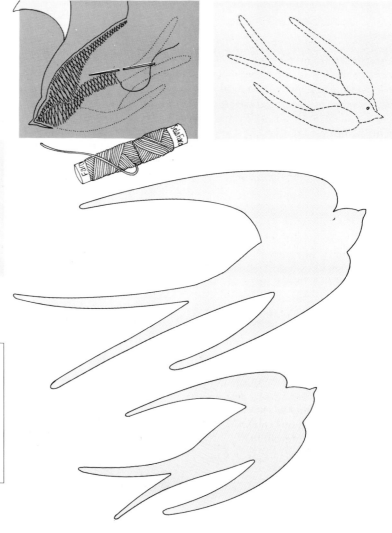

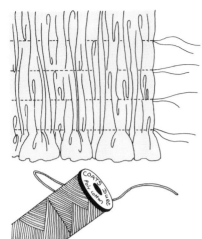

Cover press studs with a circle of lining gathered up underneath. Trim surplus fabric, place press stud in position and work but-tonhole stitch through the holes. When the press stud is closed the knob will force a hole in the fabric of the other piece.

SHIRRING

Suitable for all soft fabrics. Stitch on a large piece of fabric; the additional 5cm (2in) all round will not be sufficient. Use either sewing thread or elastic thread, the latter being much quicker to work. Wind elastic thread on to the machine bobbin, thread the machine with sewing thread on the top and set it to a large straight stitch or a running zig-zag. Stitch horizontal lines, starting on the central line on the panel and making the rows 1–2cm ($\frac{3}{8}$–$\frac{3}{4}$in) apart or – for a closer effect – use the width of the foot. Steam the shirring to contract it. If using sewing thread work parallel rows of large straight machine stitches, loosening the upper tension slightly. On the wrong side pull up all the bobbin threads, easing the fabric along evenly to ruche it.

With both methods, mark the side edges of the panel and stitch along the lines to prevent the stitches unravelling, then cut out the panel. The panel must be lined.

SMOCKING

To work the smocked centre panel, cut a piece of fabric three times the measurement, 1(a), of the top of the bodice by the depth (the measurement to be taken within the seam allowance).

Using the spots on the fabric as a guide, instead of a transfer which could be seen through on the wrong side, it is helpful to have an extra row of gathering within the seam allowance top and bottom; these remain until the garment is made up (disregard these extra gathering rows when referring to the chart). Mark the centre, which should fall between two pleats, pull the gathering threads up two at a time (2(a) on the drawing below) and secure them with pins. Work the complete oblong panel; the shape of the pattern is cut out after the smocking has been worked. The smocking design is for 15 rows; when worked twice, the rope stitch on the 15th row becomes the first. Take out the gathering threads and pin the right side onto terry towel, making sure that you check the size which should be 1(a) on the diagram. Place a piece of damp muslin over the smoking, press lightly, just allowing the steam to penetrate without pressure from the iron; leave to dry.

Next, place the pattern piece on the smocked panel, taking care that the centre front markings are matched, pin the pattern on and tack around the side edges; take off the pattern and machine twice, just inside the seam allowance. Replace the pattern and cut to shape.

The chart overleaf is for size 10, taking 29 rows of gathering for the smocked section; if on the larger sizes you have more gathering threads, increase the smocking rows as follows: if there is 1 extra, work the design of 15 rows exactly twice, giving 30 rows of smocking; if 2 extra, work 1 more top and bottom in rope stitch – 31 rows in all; if you have 3 extra, work the extra row again in rope stitch, at the top, bottom and centre – 32 rows in all; if 4 extra,

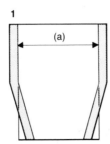

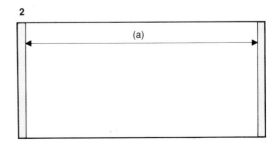

1 (a)

2 (a)

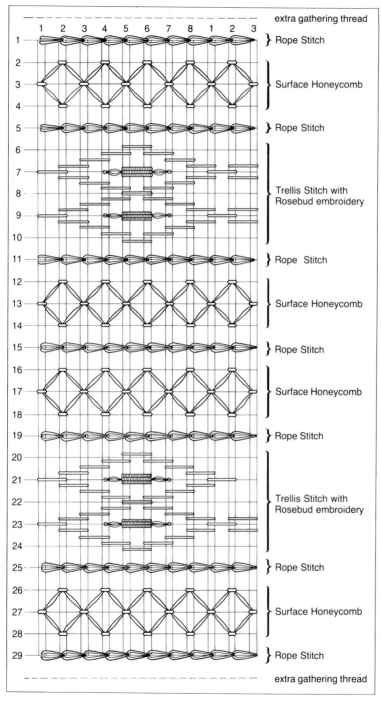

extra gathering thread

} Rope Stitch

} Surface Honeycomb

} Rope Stitch

} Trellis Stitch with Rosebud embroidery

} Rope Stitch

} Surface Honeycomb

} Rope Stitch

} Surface Honeycomb

} Rope Stitch

} Trellis Stitch with Rosebud embroidery

} Rope Stitch

} Surface Honeycomb

} Rope Stitch

extra gathering thread

increase the surface honeycomb by 1 row each time, working 4 rows instead of 3; work the rest of the smocking as the chart. It would be helpful to you to make your own chart to follow with any increased number of gathering threads.

Before starting the panel of smocking, you should work a practice piece to get an even tension and to try out all the stitches. And don't forget to start each thread with a double knot; also, don't have the thread too long, and remember to finish off with 3 overstitches worked at the back of the pleats. Finally, restart a fresh thread in the middle of a row, coming up in exactly the same place as you finished off.

SMOCKED FRILLS

Suitable for soft cottons, voile, crêpe etc., preferably spotted or striped. The panel itself is left plain but it will require backing with a piece of plain lawn or lining so that it supports the weight of the frill. Cut two lengths of fabric on the straight grain 6.5cm (2⅝in) wide and two and a half times the depth of the panel. Roll

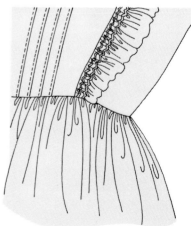

a narrow hem along one edge and slip hem. Insert three rows of gathering threads on the wrong side starting 2.5cm (1in) from the hem edge. A smock-gathering machine can be used for this. If using transfer dots, choose silver in preference to a colour on white fabric. Pull up the threads until the frill fits the bodice panel. If possible, select a smocking stitch, that reflects any pattern on the fabric. The illustration shows wave stitch, which echoes the diagonal self-stripe in the cotton crêpon that was used for the original sample. Use white Anchor Stranded embroidery thread or pale contrasting colours. Steam the smocking on completion. Turn in and hem one end of each frill. Place each frill right side down on the right side of the panel, tack with gathered edge level with the panel edge. Stitch, taking 1.5cm ($\frac{5}{8}$in) seam, and being careful to stitch an even distance from the smocking. Place side panels on top, right side down, and stitch again. The lower end of the frill is caught in the waist seam later. Note that the smocked frills could be made long enough to continue along each side of the neck and also down the back panel seams of the bodice.

TRAPUNTO

Suitable for all fabrics except those which are extremely transparent. Select a design and outline it on muslin or a similar soft open fabric such as voile. Baste this to the wrong side of the fabric. Stitch round the outline with hand-running stitch or a straight machine stitch. Make a second line of stitching outside the first and parallel to it. The distance between the rows depends on the thickness of yarn used for padding. On the wrong side use a bodkin to thread a strand of thick wool between the stitching, making a hole in the muslin where the ends will protrude.

This technique is particularly effective when worked as three or four lines outlining the edge of the garment; for example, the sweetheart neck or deep cuff. The dress hemline can be emphasized and weighted by the addition of one line of Trapunto.

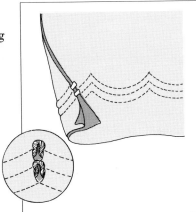

Check all your pressing equipment. You will need Vilene's Iron Cleaner for removing marks from the iron made by pressing other things; also a metre-length of butter muslin for pressing if you have not got this already. A white terry towel will be required for pressing lace. Also keep an old sheet for spreading over the floor whenever you press the skirt. Make a new cover for the ironing board, you probably need one anyway. Don't have an aluminium cover; use a piece of soft cotton or buy a piece of pale polyester/cotton sheeting. Cut a piece of foam sheet and a piece of blanket or coating fabric to exactly the shape of the board plus enough to go over the edge; attach with drawing pins or double-sided tape all round the edge.

Make the cover to fit exactly; cut a piece of fabric roughly to size and an end piece to go underneath and put them wrong side out over the board on top of the padding. Pin a well-fitting seam all round. Attach pairs of tapes to tie under the board. If any part of the edge droops, zig-zag a piece of elastic to it in order to tighten it up. If it is some years since you had a new iron, now is a good time to invest in an efficient steam iron. Should you feel this is a needless expense just now, buy one of those sole-plates that fix on to the iron with expandable wires.

Mail order suppliers and useful addresses

Buttons:

Duttons for Buttons,
32 Coppergate,
York,
N. Yorkshire

Covered buttons (also
haberdashery, including fabric pen
and basting tape):

Harlequin,
Lawling House,
Manningtree Road,
Sutton, Ipswich

Embroidery materials:

Cass Arts and Craftsmith
(Also branches at Richmond and
Slough):

The Marlows,
Hemel Hempstead,
Herts.

Fabrics:

Allans of Duke Street,
56 Duke Street,
London W1
(Tel. 01–629 3781)

Fine Dress Fabrics,
127 Crawford Street,
London W1
(Tel. 01–935 5876)

Adrian Charles Bridal Fabrics,
72 School Road,
Yardley Wood,
Birmingham B14 4JR

Various silks:

Butterfly Silks,
Acorn Fabrics Ltd.,
Union Mills,
Lower Union Street,
Skipton, Yorks BD23 2ND
(Tel. Skipton 5653)

Sussex Silks,
Horstead Keynes,
Sussex

Silk Shades,
33 Prentice Street,
Lavenham,
Suffolk CO10 9RD

Flowers, headdresses, veils,
parasols and accessories (send for
catalogue):

Kentish Maid Ltd,
18 Ramsgate Road,
Broadstairs,
Kent,
(Tel. Thanet 584909)

Hand-painting on fabric:

Anna Steiner,
Unit H,
51 Calthorpe Street,
London N1

Invisible mending:

British Invisible Mending Service,
32 Thayer Street,
London W1M 5LH
(Tel. 01–487 4292)

Pleating:

Ciment Ltd,
Wells Mews,
Wells Street,
London W1

Sewing and embroidery threads
Also haberdashery (Send £1 for
colour catalogue):

Christine Riley,
53 Barclay Street,
Stonehaven,
Kincardineshire AB3 2AR

Shoes:

Anello and Davide,
30 Drury Lane,
London WC2
(Tel. 01–836 6744)
Will dye their white satin shoes.

Gamba (sell satin shoes,
will also make):

3 Garrick Street,
London WC2
(Tel. 01–437 0704)

Silk net for mounting veils etc:

Kaplovitch Fabrics,
43 Vicarage Lane,
London E15
(Tel. 01–534 3725)

Specialist cleaners of wedding
dresses and veils (also postal
service):

Marie Blanche Laundry,
154 Battersea Park Road,
London SW11
(Tel. 01–622 0151)

Wedding veils, refurbishing:

Liberty's (wedding dress
department), Regent Street,
London W1
(Tel. 01–734 1234)

WEDDING DRESSES

Bodices		8	10	12	14	16
Panel bodice	90cm	1m	1m	1m	1·05m	1·05m
	36in	$1\frac{1}{4}$y	$1\frac{1}{4}$y	$1\frac{1}{4}$y	$1\frac{1}{4}$y	$1\frac{1}{4}$y
	115cm	70cm	70cm	75cm	80cm	90cm
	45in	1y	1y	1y	1y	1y
	Vilene 25cm/$\frac{1}{3}$y					
	Remember: buttons and thread; 40cm/16in zip; and 18cm/7 in zip for design 4					
Fitted bodice	90cm	55cm	55cm	55cm	55cm	60cm
	36in	$\frac{2}{3}$y	$\frac{2}{3}$y	$\frac{2}{3}$y	$\frac{2}{3}$y	$\frac{2}{3}$y
	115cm	55cm	55cm	55cm	55cm	60cm
	45in	$\frac{2}{3}$y	$\frac{2}{3}$y	$\frac{2}{3}$y	$\frac{2}{3}$y	$\frac{2}{3}$y
	Vilene 25cm/$\frac{1}{3}$y					
	Rigilene boning 1·2m/$1\frac{1}{3}$y; 40cm/16in zip; thread					
V-neck bodice	90cm	1·2m	1·2m	1·25m	1·3m	1·35m
	36in	$1\frac{1}{3}$y	$1\frac{1}{3}$y	$1\frac{3}{8}$y	$1\frac{3}{8}$y	$1\frac{1}{2}$y
	115cm	1m	1m	1·05m	1·05m	1·05m
	45in	$1\frac{1}{8}$y	$1\frac{1}{8}$y	$1\frac{1}{8}$y	$1\frac{1}{8}$y	$1\frac{1}{8}$y
	Remember: thread; 40cm/16in zip					
Plain bodice – slash neck	90cm	1·05m	1·1m	1·1m	1·15m	1·2m
	36in	1y	$1\frac{1}{4}$y	$1\frac{1}{4}$y	$1\frac{1}{4}$y	$1\frac{3}{8}$y
	115cm	95cm	1m	1m	1m	1·05m
	45in	1y	$1\frac{1}{8}$y	$1\frac{1}{8}$y	$1\frac{1}{8}$y	$1\frac{1}{8}$y
	Elastic 5mm/$\frac{1}{4}$in × round arm measurement twice					
	Remember: 5 buttons; 40cm/16in zip					

Sleeves		8	10	12	14	16
Long fitted sleeve	90cm	70cm	70cm	70cm	70cm	75cm
	36in	1y	1y	1y	1y	1y
	115cm	70cm	70cm	70cm	70cm	75cm
	45in	1y	1y	1y	1y	1y
	Remember: 10 buttons					
Long sleeve with shaped cuff	90cm	1·3m	1·3m	1·3m	1·3m	1·35m
	36in	$1\frac{2}{3}$y	$1\frac{2}{3}$y	$1\frac{2}{3}$y	$1\frac{2}{3}$y	$1\frac{2}{3}$y
	115cm	1·3m	1·3m	1·3m	1·3m	1·35m
	45in	$1\frac{2}{3}$y	$1\frac{2}{3}$y	$1\frac{2}{3}$y	$1\frac{2}{3}$y	$1\frac{2}{3}$y
	Vilene	25cm	25cm	25cm	25cm	25cm
		$\frac{1}{3}$y	$\frac{1}{3}$y	$\frac{1}{3}$y	$\frac{1}{3}$y	$\frac{1}{3}$y
	Remember: 6–8 buttons					

WEDDING DRESSES

Sleeves		8	10	12	14	16
Elbow-length sleeve	90cm	1m	1m	1m	1m	1·05m
	36in	$1\frac{1}{8}$y	$1\frac{1}{8}$y	$1\frac{1}{8}$y	$1\frac{1}{8}$y	$1\frac{1}{8}$y
	115cm	1m	1m	1m	1m	1·05m
	45in	$1\frac{1}{8}$y	$1\frac{1}{8}$y	$1\frac{1}{8}$y	$1\frac{1}{8}$y	$1\frac{1}{8}$y
	Elastic 5mm/$\frac{1}{4}$in × round arm measurement twice					
Below-elbow sleeve	90cm	1·1m	1·1m	1·1m	1·1m	1·15m
	36in	$1\frac{1}{3}$y	$1\frac{1}{3}$y	$1\frac{1}{3}$y	$1\frac{1}{3}$y	$1\frac{1}{3}$y
	115cm	1·1	1·1	1·1	1·1	1·15m
	45in	$1\frac{1}{3}$y	$1\frac{1}{3}$y	$1\frac{1}{3}$y	$1\frac{1}{3}$y	$1\frac{1}{4}$y
	Elastic 5mm/$\frac{1}{4}$in × round arm measurement twice					
Short sleeve with pleat or band	90cm	80cm	80cm	80cm	80cm	80cm
	36in	1y	1y	1y	1y	1y
	115cm	80cm	80cm	80cm	80cm	80cm
	45in	1y	1y	1y	1y	1y
	Elastic, Design 3: 5mm/$\frac{1}{4}$in × round arm measurement twice					
Long sleeve with narrow cuff	90cm	1·45m	1·45m	1·45m	1·45m	1·45m
	36in	$1\frac{3}{4}$y	$1\frac{3}{4}$y	$1\frac{3}{4}$y	$1\frac{3}{4}$y	$1\frac{3}{4}$y
	115cm	1·45m	1·45m	1·45m	1·45m	1·45m
	45in	$1\frac{3}{4}$y	$1\frac{3}{4}$y	$1\frac{3}{4}$y	$1\frac{3}{4}$y	$1\frac{3}{4}$y
	Fold-a-band (cuff weight) 50cm/20in					
$\frac{3}{4}$ length slashed sleeve	95cm	95cm	1m	1m	1m	1·05m
	36in	$1\frac{1}{8}$y	$1\frac{1}{8}$y	$1\frac{1}{8}$y	$1\frac{1}{8}$y	$1\frac{1}{4}$y
	115cm	95cm	1m	1m	1m	1·05m
	45in	$1\frac{1}{8}$y	$1\frac{1}{8}$y	$1\frac{1}{8}$y	$1\frac{1}{8}$y	$1\frac{1}{4}$y
Elbow-length sleeve with cap	90cm	1·2m	1·25m	1·3m	1·3m	1·3m
	36in	$1\frac{1}{2}$y	$1\frac{1}{2}$y	$1\frac{2}{3}$y	$1\frac{2}{3}$y	$1\frac{2}{3}$y
	115cm	1m	1m	1m	1·05m	1·05m
	45in	$1\frac{1}{4}$y	$1\frac{1}{4}$y	$1\frac{1}{4}$y	$1\frac{1}{3}$y	$1\frac{1}{3}$y
	Elastic 5mm/$\frac{1}{4}$in × round arm measurement twice					
Elbow-length sleeve with contrast cap	90cm	1·1m	1·1m	1·1m	1·1m	1·15m
	36in	$1\frac{1}{3}$y	$1\frac{1}{3}$y	$1\frac{1}{3}$y	$1\frac{1}{3}$y	$1\frac{1}{3}$y
	115cm	1·1m	1·1m	1·1m	1·1m	1·15m
	45in	$1\frac{1}{3}$y	$1\frac{1}{3}$y	$1\frac{1}{3}$y	$1\frac{1}{3}$y	$1\frac{1}{3}$y
Cap	90cm	25cm	25cm	30cm	30cm	30cm
	36in	$\frac{1}{3}$y	$\frac{1}{3}$y	$\frac{1}{3}$y	$\frac{1}{3}$y	$\frac{1}{3}$y
	115cm	20cm	20cm	20cm	25cm	25cm
	45in	$\frac{1}{4}$y	$\frac{1}{4}$y	$\frac{1}{4}$y	$\frac{1}{3}$y	$\frac{1}{3}$y
	Elastic 5mm/$\frac{1}{4}$in × round arm measurement twice					

WEDDING DRESSES

Skirt		8	10	12	14	16
8 panels, full-length	90cm	9·45m	9·45m	9·45m	9·45m	9·45m
	36in	10¼y	10¼y	10¼y	10¼y	10¼y
	115cm	9·45m	9·45m	9·45m	9·45m	9·45m
	45in	10¼y	10¼y	10¼y	10¼y	10¼y
6 panels, full-length	90cm	7·05m	7·05m	7·05m	7·05m	7·05m
	36in	7⅔y	7⅔y	7⅔y	7⅔y	7⅔y
	115cm	7·05m	7·05m	7·05m	7·05m	7·05m
	45in	7⅔y	7⅔y	7⅔y	7⅔y	7⅔y
4 panels, full-length	90cm	4·7m	4·7m	4·7m	4·7m	4·7m
	36in	5⅓y	5⅓y	5⅓y	5⅓y	5⅓y
	115cm	4·7m	4·7m	4·7m	4·7m	4·7m
	45in	5⅓y	5⅓y	5⅓y	5⅓y	5⅓

Petticoats: follow skirt quantities
Remember: 1m/1y narrow tape for waistline; 40cm/16in zip for the side; 4–6 reels of thread for each dress

		8	10	12	14	16
6 panels, with frill	90cm	10m	10m	10m	10m	10m
	36in	11y	11y	11y	11y	11y
	115cm	10m	10m	10m	10m	10m
	45in	11y	11y	11y	11y	11y
6 panels, underskirt	90cm	10m	10m	10m	10m	10m
	36in	11y	11y	11y	11y	11y
	115cm	10m	10m	10m	10m	10m
	45in	11y	11y	11y	11y	11y
8 panels, overskirt	90cm	8·4m	8·4m	8·4m	8·4m	8·4m
	36in	9⅛y	9⅛y	9⅛y	9⅛y	9⅛y
	115cm	8·4m	8·4m	8·4m	8·4m	8·4m
	45in	9⅛y	9⅛y	9⅛y	9⅛y	9⅛y

Or: 16m/17⅓y if all one fabric

		8	10	12	14	16
Tiered skirt, 3 tiers	90cm	12·4m	12·4m	12·4m	12·4m	12·4m
	36in	13y	13y	13y	13y	13y
	115cm	12·4m	12·4m	12·4m	12·4m	12·4m
	45in	13y	13y	13y	13y	13y
Short skirt, with frill	90cm	4·1m	4·1m	4·1m	4·1m	4·1m
	36in	4⅔y	4⅔y	4⅔y	4⅔y	4⅔y
	115cm	4·1m	4·1m	4·1m	4·1m	4·1m
	45in	4⅔y	4⅔y	4⅔y	4⅔y	4⅔y
Short skirt, 6 panels	90cm	5m	5m	5m	5m	5m
	36in	5⅔y	5⅔y	5⅔y	5⅔y	5⅔y
	115cm	5m	5m	5m	5m	5m
	45in	5⅔y	5⅔y	5⅔y	5⅔y	5⅔y

WEDDING DRESSES

Skirt		8	10	12	14	16
8 floating panels	90cm	5·6m	5·6m	5·6m	5·6m	5·6m
	36in	6¼y	6¼y	6¼y	6¼y	6¼y
	115cm	5·6m	5·6m	5·6m	5·6m	5·6m
	45in	6¼y	6¼y	6¼y	6¼y	6¼y
	Or: 10·5m/11½y if all one fabric					
Short tiered skirt	90cm	8·5m	8·5m	8·5m	8·5m	8·5m
	36in	9¼y	9¼y	9¼y	9¼y	9¼y
	115cm	8·5m	8·5m	8·5m	8·5m	8·5m
	45in	9¼y	9¼y	9¼y	9¼y	9¼y
Long skirt, double frills	90cm	11·7m	11·7m	11·7m	11·7m	11·7m
	36in	12⅛y	12⅛y	12⅛y	12⅛y	12⅛y
	115cm	11·7m	11·7m	11·7m	11·7m	11·7m
	45in	12⅛y	12⅛y	12⅛y	12⅛y	12⅛y
	Cut 6 panels to hemline D. Cut 9 Pieces 90cm/36in long and 50cm/20in deep for underfill. Cut 9 pieces 90cm/36in long and 33cm/13in deep for upper frill.					
Long tiered skirt, 4 tiers	90cm	12·7m	12·7m	12·7m	12·7m	12·7m
	36in	13½y	13½y	13½y	13½y	13½y
	115cm	12·7m	12·7m	12·7m	12·7m	12·7m
	45in	13½y	13½y	13½y	13½y	13½y
	Cut 4 panels to hemline C. Cut 6 pieces 90cm/36in long and 24cm/9¾ deep for waist peplum. Cut 7 pieces 90cm/36in long and 29cm/11½in deep for second tier. Cut 8 pieces 90cm/36in long and 38cm/15in deep for third tier. Cut 9 pieces 90cm/36in long and 39cm/15½in deep for hemline frill. Stitch second tier to placement line; stitch third tier to line E.					

Features and Accessories		8	10	12	14	16
Shoulder frill, single	90cm	2m	2m	2m	2m	2m
	36in	2¼y	2¼y	2¼y	2¼y	1¼y
	115cm	2m	2m	2m	2m	2m
	45cm	2¼y	2¼y	2¼y	2¼y	2¼y
	Remember: add quantity for bodice if all one fabric					
Shoulder frill, double	90cm	2m	2m	2m	2m	2m
	36in	2¼y	2¼y	2¼y	2¼y	2¼y
	115cm	2m	2m	2m	2m	2m
	45cm	2¼y	2¼y	2¼y	2¼y	2¼y
	Remember: add quantity for bodice if all one fabric					
Neckline flounce, single	90cm	2·7m	2·7m	2·7m	2·7m	2·7m
	36in	3y	3y	3y	3y	3y
	115cm	2·7m	2·7m	2·7m	2·7m	2·7m
	45cm	3y	3y	3y	3y	3y
	2m/2¼y narrow elastic or 1 spool shirring elastic *Remember*: add quantity for bodice if all one fabric					

WEDDING DRESSES

Features and Accessories		8	10	12	14	16
Neckline flounce, double	**90cm**	2·7m	2·7m	2·7m	2·7m	2·7m
	36in	3y	3y	3y	3y	3y
	115cm	2·7m	2·7m	2·7m	2·7m	2·7m
	45in	3y	3y	3y	3y	3y

2m/2¼y narrow elastic or 1 spool shirring elastic
Remember: add quantity for bodice if all one fabric

Accessory metreage if buying specifically

Fabric and Haberdashery

Dolly bag	**90cm**	90cm
	36in	1m
	115cm	90cm
	45in	1m
Clutch bag	**90cm**	60cm
	36in	¾y
	115cm	60cm
	45in	¾y
Bridesmaid's purse	**90cm**	30cm
	36in	⅓y
	115cm	30cm
	45in	⅓y
Muff	**90cm**	60cm
	36in	¾y
	115cm	60cm
	45in	¾y
Swallow	**90 (36)** / **115 (45)**	25cm / ⅓y
Adult sash	**90 (36)** / **115 (45)**	2·05m / 2¼y
Belt	**90 (36)** / **115(45)**	90cm / 1y
Belt: Pelmet Vilene	**90 (36)** / **115 (45)**	10cm / ¼y
Cummerbund	**90 (36)** / **115 (45)**	1m / 1¼y
Cummerbund: pelmet Vilene	**90 (36)** / **115 (45)**	15cm / ¼y
Swallow: Wadding	**90 (36)** / **115 (45)**	15cm / ¼y

WEDDING DRESSES

Fabric and Haberdashery		8	10	12	14	16
Train	**90cm**	1·5m	1·5m	1·5m	1·5m	1·5m
	36in	1½y	1½y	1½y	1½y	1½y
	115cm	1·5m	1·5m	1·5m	1·5m	1·5m
	45in	1½y	1½y	1½y	1½y	1½y
Train hemline frill	**90cm**	85cm	85cm	85cm	85cm	85cm
	36in	1y	1y	1y	1y	1y
	115cm	85cm	85cm	85cm	85cm	85cm
	45in	1y	1y	1y	1y	1y
Train frill for centre of train	**90cm**	3m	3m	3m	3m	3m
	36in	3¼y	3¼y	3¼y	¼y	¼y
	115cm	3m	3m	3m	3m	3m
	45in	3¼y	3¼y	3¼y	3¼y	3¼y

TROUSSEAU

Kimono		S Long	S Short	M Long	M Short	L Long	L Short
Kimono and lining in same fabric	**90cm**	9·2m	6·5m	9·3m	6·6m	9·4m	6·6m
	36in	10y	7y	10¼y	7¼y	10¼y	7¼y
	115cm	8·8m	6·05m	8·85m	6·1m	8·95m	6·2m
	45in	9⅔y	6⅔y	9⅔y	6⅔y	9¾y	6¾y
Sash	**90cm**	2·05m	2·05m	2·05m	2·05m	2·05m	2·05m
	36in	2¼y	2¼y	2¼y	2¼y	2¼y	2¼y
	115cm	2·05m	2·05m	2·05m	2·05m	2·05m	2·05m
	45in	2¼y	2¼y	2¼y	2¼y	2¼y	2¼y

Kimono with bands and lining in contrast fabric		S Long	S Short	M Long	M Short	L Long	L Short
Bands, front and sleeves	**90cm**	4·4m	3·05m	4·45m	3·1m	4·5m	3·1m
	36in	5y	3⅓y	5¼y	3½y	5¼y	3½y
	115cm	4·4m	3·05m	4·45m	3·1m	4·5m	3·1m
	45in	5y	3⅓y	5¼y	3½y	5¼y	3½y
Contrast for front bands, sleeve bands and lining	**90cm**	5·35m	4·6m	5·4m	4·6m	5·45	4.65m
	36in	6y	5¼y	6y	5¼y	6y	5¼y
	115cm	4·6m	4·65m	4·65m	3·3m	4·65	3·3m
	45in	5¼y	3⅔y	5¼y	3¾y	5¼y	3¾y

All-in-one		S	M	L
	90cm	2m	2·05m	2·05m
	36in	2¼y	2¼y	2¼y
	115cm	1·6m	1·7m	1·95
	45in	1¾y	2y	2¼y

TROUSSEAU

All-in-one with contrast colour bands and straps		S	M	L
Body sections	90cm	1·6m	1·6m	1·65m
	36in	1¾y	1¾y	2y
	115cm	1·25m	1·35m	1·6m
	45in	1⅓y	1½y	1¾y
Contrast for bands and straps	90cm	70cm	75cm	80cm
	36in	1y	1y	1y
	115cm	70cm	75cm	80cm
	45in	1y	1y	1y

Elastic: Waist measurement; 2 reels thread; 1m/1⅛y narrow ribbon if required; lace if required

BRIDESMAID'S DRESSES

Bodices		5	6	7	8	9	10
Plain bodice with double collar or frill (high and low neck)	90cm	30cm	35cm	35cm	40cm	45cm	50cm
	36in	⅓y	½y	½y	½y	½y	⅔y
	115cm	30cm	35cm	35cm	40cm	40cm	40cm
	45in	⅓y	½y	½y	½y	½y	½y

30cm/12in zip

Panel bodice (round and square neck)	90cm	70cm	70cm	75cm	75cm	80cm	85cm
	36in	1y	1y	1y	1y	1y	1y
	115cm	50cm	50cm	50cm	55cm	60cm	60cm
	45in	⅔y	⅔y	⅔y	⅔y	⅔y	⅔y

30cm/12in zip; 20cm/¼y Vilene (all sizes)

Sleeves		5	6	7	8	9	10
Long sleeve	90cm	50cm	55cm	55cm	1·15m	1·2m	1·2m
	36in	⅔y	⅔y	⅔y	1⅓y	1½y	1½y
	115cm	50cm	55cm	55cm	60cm	60cm	60cm
	45in	⅔y	⅔y	⅔y	⅔y	⅔y	⅔y

Elastic: 3 × waist measurement, 6 × waist measurement, or 1 reel shirring elastic

Short sleeve	90cm	30cm	30cm	30cm	60cm	65cm	65cm
	36in	⅓y	⅓y	⅓y	⅔y	¾y	¾y
	115cm	30cm	30cm	30cm	30cm	30cm	35cm
	45in	⅓y	⅓y	⅓y	⅓y	⅓y	½y
Cap only	90cm	15cm	15cm	20cm	20cm	20cm	20cm
	36in	¼y	¼y	¼y	¼y	¼y	¼y
	115cm	15cm	15cm	15cm	15cm	15cm	15cm
	45in	¼y	¼y	¼y	¼y	¼y	¼y

BRIDESMAID'S DRESSES

Collar if using contrast fabric		5	6	7	8	9	10
Lower collar	90cm	25cm	25cm	30cm	30cm	30cm	30cm
	36in	$\frac{1}{3}$y	$\frac{1}{3}$y	$\frac{1}{3}$y	$\frac{1}{3}$y	$\frac{1}{3}$y	$\frac{1}{3}$y
	115cm	15cm	15cm	15cm	15cm	15cm	15cm
	45in	$\frac{1}{4}$y	$\frac{1}{4}$y	$\frac{1}{4}$y	$\frac{1}{4}$y	$\frac{1}{4}$y	$\frac{1}{4}$y
	Vilene: 15cm/$\frac{1}{4}$y						
Upper collar	90cm	25cm	25cm	25cm	25cm	25cm	25cm
	36in	$\frac{1}{3}$y	$\frac{1}{3}$y	$\frac{1}{3}$y	$\frac{1}{3}$y	$\frac{1}{3}$y	$\frac{1}{3}$y
	115cm	15cm	15cm	15cm	15cm	15cm	15cm
	45in	$\frac{1}{4}$y	$\frac{1}{4}$y	$\frac{1}{4}$y	$\frac{1}{4}$y	$\frac{1}{4}$y	$\frac{1}{4}$y
	Vilene: 15cm/$\frac{1}{4}$y						

Skirts		5	6	7	8	9	10
Long plain	90cm	1·5m	1·55m	1·65m	1·75m	1·9m	2m
	36in	$1\frac{3}{4}$y	$1\frac{3}{4}$y	2y	$2\frac{1}{4}$y	$2\frac{1}{8}$y	$2\frac{1}{8}$y
	115cm	1·5m	1·55m	1·65m	1·75m	1·9m	2m
	45in	$1\frac{3}{4}$y	$1\frac{3}{4}$y	2y	$2\frac{1}{4}$y	$2\frac{1}{8}$y	$2\frac{1}{8}$y
Long with frill	90cm	1·95m	1·95m	2·05m	2·05m	2·1m	2·15m
	36in	$2\frac{1}{8}$y	$2\frac{1}{8}$y	$2\frac{1}{3}$y	$2\frac{2}{3}$y	$2\frac{1}{3}$y	$2\frac{1}{3}$y
	115cm	1·95m	1·95m	2·05m	2·05m	2·1m	2·15m
	45in	$2\frac{1}{8}$y	$2\frac{1}{8}$y	$2\frac{1}{3}$y	$2\frac{1}{3}$y	$2\frac{1}{3}$y	$2\frac{1}{3}$y
Short plain	90cm	90cm	90cm	95cm	1m	1m	1.05m
	36in	1y	1y	$1\frac{1}{4}$y	$1\frac{1}{4}$y	$1\frac{1}{4}$y	$1\frac{1}{4}$y
	115cm	90cm	90cm	95cm	1m	1m	1.5m
	45in	1y	1y	$1\frac{1}{4}$y	$1\frac{1}{4}$y	$1\frac{1}{4}$y	$1\frac{1}{4}$y
Long skirt with peplum	90cm	1·95m	2m	2·1m	2·3m	2·5m	2·6m
	36in	$2\frac{1}{4}$y	$2\frac{1}{8}$y	$2\frac{1}{3}$y	$2\frac{1}{3}$y	3y	$3\frac{1}{4}$y
	115cm	1·95m	2m	2·1m	2·3m	2·5m	2·6m
	45in	$2\frac{1}{4}$y	$2\frac{1}{8}$y	$2\frac{1}{3}$y	$2\frac{2}{3}$y	3y	$3\frac{1}{4}$y
Long skirt with frill and peplum	90cm	2·5m	2·55m	2·6m	2·65m	2·7m	2·75m
	36in	3y	3y	$3\frac{1}{4}$y	$3\frac{1}{4}$y	$3\frac{1}{4}$y	$3\frac{1}{4}$y
	115cm	2·5m	2·55m	2·6m	2·65m	2·7m	2·75m
	45in	3y	3y	$3\frac{1}{4}$y	$3\frac{1}{4}$y	$3\frac{1}{4}$y	$3\frac{1}{4}$y
	Petticoat: as skirt quantities						

Shoulder frills for panel bodice		5	6	7	8	9	10
Single	90cm	1·45m	1·45m	1·45m	1·45m	1·45m	1·45m
	36in	1y	1y	1y	1y	1y	1y
	115cm	1·45m	1·45m	1·45m	1·45m	1·45m	1·45
	45in	1y	1y	1y	1y	1y	1y

BRIDESMAID'S DRESSES

Shoulder frills for panel bodice		5	6	7	8	9	10
Double	90cm	1·45m	1·45m	1·45m	1·45m	1·45m	1·45m
	36in	1y	1y	1y	1y	1y	1y
	115cm	1·45m	1·45m	1·45m	1·45m	1·45m	1·45m
	45in	1y	1y	1y	1y	1y	1y
Sash	90cm	1m	1m	1m	1m	1m	1m
	36in	$1\frac{1}{4}$y	$1\frac{1}{4}$y	$1\frac{1}{4}$y	$1\frac{1}{4}$y	$1\frac{1}{4}$y	$1\frac{1}{4}$y
	115cm	1m	1m	1m	1m	1m	1m
	45in	$1\frac{1}{4}$y	$1\frac{1}{4}$	$1\frac{1}{4}$	$1\frac{1}{4}$	$1\frac{1}{4}$	$1\frac{1}{4}$

Remember: buy at least 3 reels of thread for each dress

Note: Decide on the design you want and add together the quantities of fabric quoted above. Although you may be able to economise by laying out all pattern pieces and dovetailing them to cut out, don't forget you will need extra fabric for trying out stitches and decorative processes. Also remember to allow extra if you intend to do smocking, shirring, ruching etc.

PATTERN SIZES

The paper patterns are cut to the following sizes. The measurements include ease for movement. Select your usual size, remembering to check and adjust sleeve and skirt lengths if necessary, before cutting out in fabric

Adult patterns	8	10	12	14	16	
Bust	80cm	83cm	87cm	92cm	97cm	
	$31\frac{1}{2}$in	$32\frac{1}{2}$in	34in	36in	38in	
Waist	61cm	64cm	67cm	71cm	76cm	
	24in	25in	$26\frac{1}{2}$in	28in	30in	
Hips	85cm	88cm	92cm	97cm	102cm	
	$33\frac{1}{2}$in	$34\frac{1}{2}$in	36in	38in	40in	
Back neck to waist	40cm	40·5cm	41·5cm	42cm	42·5cm	
	$15\frac{3}{4}$	16in	$16\frac{1}{4}$in	$16\frac{1}{2}$in	$16\frac{3}{4}$in	
Skirt length to ankle	108cm	108cm	108cm	108cm	108	
	$42\frac{1}{2}$in	$42\frac{1}{2}$in	$42\frac{1}{2}$in	$42\frac{1}{2}$in	$42\frac{1}{2}$in	
Skirt length below knee	70·5cm	70·5cm	70·5cm	70·5cm	70·5cm	
	$27\frac{3}{4}$in	$27\frac{3}{4}$in	$27\frac{3}{4}$in	$27\frac{3}{4}$in	$27\frac{3}{4}$in	

Children's Patterns	5	6	7	8	9	10
Chest	64cm	66·5cm	69cm	71cm	73cm	74·5cm
	25in	26in	27in	$27\frac{1}{2}$in	$28\frac{1}{2}$in	29in
Waist	56cm	58cm	60cm	61cm	62cm	63·5cm
	22in	$22\frac{1}{2}$in	$23\frac{1}{2}$in	24in	$24\frac{1}{2}$in	25in
Hips	66cm	68·5cm	71cm	73·5cm	76cm	78·5
	26in	27in	28in	29in	30in	31in
Back neck to hem – full length	88cm	94cm	105cm	107cm	114cm	120·5cm
	$34\frac{1}{2}$in	37in	$41\frac{1}{4}$in	42in	45in	$47\frac{1}{2}$in
Back neck to hem – short	58·5cm	62cm	65cm	68cm	71cm	73cm
	23in	$24\frac{1}{2}$in	$25\frac{1}{2}$in	$26\frac{3}{4}$in	28in	29in

Style details for basic designs

Dress design no. 1

The panelled bodice with a full sleeve gathered into the deep cuff. The bodice fastens with one button at the top of the centre back seam. The skirt has six panels.

Suitable for crisp fabrics. Use decorative techniques on bodice centre panel and cuffs.

(back)

Dress design no. 2

The panelled bodice with full sleeve to below elbow with elastic casing. The bodice fastens with five buttons and loops at the back

(back)

seam. The skirt has six panels cut to shorter length with deep frill attached.

Use crisp fabrics, adding bows, piping, rosettes etc.

Dress design no. 3

The panelled bodice with wide, shaped frill bound and set into back and front seams. The full sleeve to short length with elastic in casing. The overskirt is made of 8 panels caught up at the seams, the underlayer has 6 panels but with deep frill. The back bodice has a deep square neck.

Suitable for crisp fabrics or a combination of different textures. Bind the bodice seams, and add bows or rosettes to overskirt.

(back)

Dress design no. 4

The panelled bodice with sweetheart neck, sleeve fitted and buttoned from elbow to wrist. The back bodice has a short zip in the centre back seam. The skirt has 4 panels, probably sufficient for velvet but add more if you wish.

Suitable for velvet, brocade and other medium-weighted textured fabrics. Use contrast for buttons, loops, piping etc.

(back)

Dress design no. 5

The fitted bodice and full length tiered skirt with single or double shoulder flounce. The flounce is stitched to the shoulder straps for security but if you wish to wear it off the shoulders later, the straps could be removed. Use soft fabric such as voile, georgette, lace etc., Alternatively if the wedding dress is made from cotton fabric it could be dyed afterwards, perhaps adding a different flounce. The skirt panels are covered by frills so lining or plain cotton material could be used for their panels.

(back)

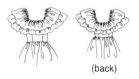

(back)

Dress design no. 6

The blouson bodice with short sleeves with band cuffs, V-neck with facing finished on the outside. The skirt is made up of four panels, or more if you wish, with deep hemline frill. The facing and sleeve bands can be decorated. You can make a matching belt or cummerbund. Work the decoration before cutting pieces exactly to size.

Use soft or crisp plain or figured fabrics. Neck and sleeve bands could be made in a contrasting colour or texture.

(back)

Dress design no. 7

The blouson bodice with elbow length sleeves and skirt of floating panels made in a see-through fabric. The underdress is made from the fitted bodice with calf length skirt. The sleeves have elastic in the hems, the slash neckline is bound and the dress fastens on the shoulder with 5 small buttons and rouleau loops made from contrast fabric or fabric of underdress. The waistline is elasticated. Layers can feature contrasting colours as well as textures. Edge the overskirt panels with fine decorative machine stitching.

(back)

Dress design no. 8

Full length strapless petticoat or evening dress from fitted bodice pattern with a skirt made of 6 panels or more or less if you wish.

Suitable for soft or crisp fabrics, plain or figured.

(back)

Dress design no. 9

Fitted bodice with three-tiered short skirt that can be made as an underdress or as a sundress. It could be made in cotton material for the wedding and dyed for later use. Alternatively, make up as a honeymoon dress in plain or figured soft or crisp fabric, even using contrasting colours.

(back)

Bridesmaid's dress design No. 1

The plain bodice has a collar and long sleeves, centre back zip and short-length skirt.

This could be made from velvet, plain or figured cottons, with contrasting double collar.

(back)

Bridesmaid's dress design No. 2

The plain bodice has a bound and frilled neckline, short puffed sleeves and centre back zip. The skirt is full-length with a deep hemline frill.

Use soft or crisp fabrics that gather well, such as taffeta.

(back)

Bridesmaid's dress design No. 3

The square panelled bodice with short puffed sleeves and centre back zip. The skirt is full-length with a peplum gathered into the waist.

Use crisp or soft fabrics or combine contrasting colours and textures, for example figured voils over plain cotton

A variation of the panelled bodice with shoulder frills set into the seams.

(back)

Kimono

A romantic but practical robe in traditional kimono style. The back, front and sleeves are cut from the simple rectangles shown on page 67. It can be made either knee-length or full-length and belted with the long sash or cummerbund. Line the kimono with self fabric or contrast.

Use plain or patterned silk, satin, crêpe de chine, tussah or soft or crisp cotton.

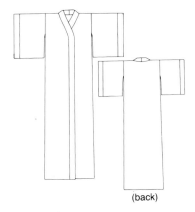

(back)

All-in-one

Nightwear or holiday suit with elastic waist and right-side facing bands round the top and legs. It has wide straps and fastens at the back with ribbon or rouleau ties. Follow the diagram pattern on page 70.

Use lingerie satin or crêpe de chine or bright cotton with contrast bands.

(back)

Index